"An innovative, effective system for creating content that delivers the one thing every audience craves: relevancy. Highly recommended!"

JAY BAER, Founder of Convince & Convert
and author of *Youtility*

"*The Content Fuel Framework* delivers on its promise: Melanie's system will ignite new ideas for getting your message out, and get you fired up to create content in ways you'd never even considered."

JOHN LEE DUMAS, Founder and Host, Entrepreneurs on Fire

"Marketing doesn't need another content marketing book. But we *do* need a practical, accessible, ridiculously useful guide to reimagining our great ideas in a hundred different ways (literally!). *The Content Fuel Framework* should come packaged with every 2020 marketing plan. Highly recommend!"

ANN HANDLEY, Chief Content Officer, MarketingProfs and
Wall Street Journal best-selling author of *Everybody Writes*

"Melanie Deziel's book, *The Content Fuel Framework*, is exactly what businesses need today to get noticed. I've published over 6000 pieces of content online, and I'm not sure I'd publish another tweet without spending more time deep in her words. You should too."

MITCH JOEL, author of *Six Pixels of Separation*
and *CTRL ALT Delete*

"The most dreaded question for any content creator is 'what should I talk about?' In this book Melanie not only makes this question into a joy to answer, but she does it through an incredibly powerful and easy to understand framework. If true creativity is the engine we must fuel, Melanie's framework is the simple instructions that can help us all drill for oil."

ROBERT ROSE, Chief Strategy Officer,
TCA: The Content Advisory

"Content creation is a lot of work and takes great consistency to pay off. It's important to have a game plan, but knowing where to start is still the challenge. Melanie Deziel lays it all out for you in *The Content Fuel Framework*. This must-read is the guide you need to achieve the clarity to successfully catapult your ideas into the world, allowing you to present a reliable and trustworthy brand."

AMY SCHMITTAUER LANDINO, Creator of AmyTV
and author of *Good Morning, Good Life*

"Marketers struggling to create engaging content will have a savior in *The Content Fuel Framework*. The Focus + Format approach is a simple yet highly effective way to inspire numerous rich ideas to rescue any content marketing program."

LEE ODDEN, CEO and Co-Founder of TopRank Marketing

"If your content marketing tank is running low, Melanie Deziel's book will connect you to a deep and rich well of content ideas so you never run dry again."

MICHAEL STELZNER, Founder of Social Media Examiner
and Social Media Marketing World

"A marketer is only as good as their storytelling. Melanie's framework for effective content strategy development is airtight and a game changer for anyone from seasoned marketers to newbies. Meet your new secret weapon. *The Content Fuel Framework* isn't a book, it's an action plan guaranteed to take your storytelling to the next level. Get ready to unlock your most productive and impactful marketing tool yet. Don't have another content brainstorm until you've read *The Content Fuel Framework*."

KIKI VON GLINOW, CEO and Co-Founder, Toast Media Group

"In the world of content creation and marketing, it's becoming harder to stand out in today's very noisy, crowded online space. However, there is hope! Melanie Deziel has served up *the* framework we've all been looking for to help generate idea after idea, leading to a consistent stream of original, high-quality content that'll serve your niche for years to come. Dive in!"

CHRIS DUCKER, YOUpreneur

"For content practitioners, small business owners, content experts, and those starting out, Melanie Deziel offers a useful, tactical framework, including deeper questions to help generate content ideas, and smarter ways to have a plan around your content calendar. Documenting the idea generation process will help readers fine-tune content ideas, but also come up with new ways to reach audience segments, making happier, more fulfilled customers. Isn't that what it's all about? This should be a quarterly exercise for all brand marketing teams!"

CATHY MCPHILLIPS, VP of Marketing,
Content Marketing Institute

"Don't be fooled by the fact that this book is a quick and easy read ... Deziel has made the complex world of content marketing simple and clear. Her powerful content fuel framework lives up to its promise and will help readers generate 500+ content ideas in a single sitting!"

CHRIS WINFIELD, CEO and Co-Founder,
Super Connector Media

"Did you ever hear the story about the person who consistently created meaningful, compelling, and relevant content? That story starts with this book and ends with your success. Read it. Use it. And live happily ever after. If you're in the driver's seat of content creation, this book is your fuel."

RON TITE, Founder of Church+State
and author of *Think Do Say*

"Coming up with content ideas can strike fear into the heart of even the most stalwart content creators and storytellers. But Melanie has a cure for that fear: a simple system for reliably—and creatively—coming up with dozens, even hundreds, of useful, relevant, and new angles to almost any story."

TAMSEN WEBSTER, Founder and Chief Message Strategist,
Find the Red Thread

"Melanie is a pioneer in content marketing and one of the smartest minds in the game. While so many content strategy frameworks are obtuse hieroglyphics with 47 different boxes and arrows pointing to each other, *The Content Fuel Framework* is simple, accessible, and will help you start coming up with better story ideas tomorrow."

JOE LAZAUSKAS, VP of Marketing, Contently
and author of *The Storytelling Edge*

"I didn't need this book to know that Melanie Deziel is a go-to pro when it comes to content marketing and brand storytelling. But we all need the useful process she shares in *The Content Fuel Framework* to become more efficient and effective content creators."

BRIAN CLARK, Founder and CEO, Copyblogger Media

"Pay attention to Melanie's framework on how to really change the way you think about content generation. Her powerful system of Focus + Format is brilliant and will help give your stories structure. You will love this book, you'll want to share it with your team, and it will change the way you share your message with the world."

NEEN JAMES, Attention Expert and Keynote speaker, Neen James Inc.

THE
CONTENT
FUEL
FRAMEWORK

THE
CONTENT
FUEL
FRAMEWORK

How to Generate
Unlimited Story Ideas

MELANIE DEZIEL

ISBN 978-1-7343290-0-1 (paperback)
ISBN 978-1-7343290-1-8 (ebook)

Storyfuel Press

Produced by Page Two
www.pagetwo.com

Cover and interior design by Fiona Lee

www.storyfuel.co

To all the stories waiting to be told,
& all the storytellers ready to tell them

Contents

Introduction

CREATIVITY WITHIN
CONFINES

EVERY SINGLE day, more than 500,000 new websites are created. Hundreds of hours of video are uploaded to YouTube each minute. Thousands of tweets are sent each second. There are more than 700,000 podcasts, each releasing new episodes all the time.

Updated versions of these types of statistics roll out annually, and each time I see one I have the same few thoughts.

First, I think about how lucky we are to live in a time when content creation and distribution has been so thoroughly democratized. Content-creation tools and technology have never been more accessible, and the proliferation of the internet and social media has largely done away with the gatekeepers of yore, who got to decide which stories were worth telling and what content could be shared. In the present day—and for the foreseeable future—we can all be storytellers. That's a beautiful thing.

Second, I think about how content consumption has become more audience-led, due to the sheer volume of content being created. We can't possibly consume it all*, so we have to hone our expectations, raise our standards, and make tougher choices about where we spend our time. This means the pressure on creators and storytellers is higher than ever before: we must create content compelling and differentiated enough to rise to the top of an increasingly crowded content landscape.

Third, I think about the amazing opportunity that these two realities have created for the people who are willing to invest the time and effort into creating truly remarkable storytelling. I see these ever-increasing numbers as a good thing: a sign that storytellers will continue to play a role in our society.

This warms my heart, because I've always been a storyteller. As a child, one of my hobbies involved "making books." I would fold plain paper in half and fill the sheets with words, stickers, and drawings, creating booklets that offered both dramatic retellings of my experiences at school or home and completely fabricated stories about animals and aliens.[‡]

As I grew older, I became an avid reader, seeing the power stories have to transport audiences and teach lessons. I excelled in English and literature courses and jumped at every chance to hone my storytelling skills: I wrote for my middle school yearbook, edited my high school literary

---

* I periodically need to declare "content bankruptcy" by clearing my podcast queue, unsubscribing myself from email newsletters, and donating a stack of unread best-sellers from my overflowing bookshelf.

‡ While this is my first published book, "Kiki the Ballerina," presented in Crayola crayon and glitter stickers, was probably my true debut work.

magazine, and served as the editor in chief of my school news publications in middle school, high school, college, and graduate school.*

Ultimately, it was journalism that captured my heart. I saw each article and assignment as a chance to become an expert on a new topic, to learn and share someone else's story, and to use my talents to help efficiently share knowledge with others. To me, a life of telling stories this way seemed like a dream come true.

But I know that not everyone shares the same excitement about a future of rampant content creation and increased storytelling. For some—especially those who have had content creation or production added to their already-filled work plates—each new social platform that launches or each new content format that catches on is an overwhelming reminder of the work to be done, and the increasingly hungry audiences we need to continue to feed with quality content.

Where will the ideas come from, we ask ourselves. We've been conditioned—through ancient myths, modern movie plot lines, dramatic entrepreneur origin stories—to believe that creativity and inspiration are either innate or random.

Some people, it seems, are just born with it. For those folks—the ones lucky enough to come into this world with some special creative ability—the ideas flow freely. They surface radical new concepts, introduce revolutionary new products, disrupt entire industries, and change the way we think. These people are labeled "creative geniuses" and are put up on a pedestal, elevating them to superhuman status. Leonardo da Vinci. Marie Curie. Steve Jobs. Beyoncé.

---

* Shoutout to the St. Francis Forum, Sacred Heart High School Forum, University of Connecticut Daily Campus, and Syracuse University NewsHouse.

For others, great ideas seem to come as a stroke of luck. Things, people, or circumstances line up *just right* for them to make a discovery or use an object in an entirely new way. The Swiss engineer George de Mestral invented the hook-and-loop fastening system now known as Velcro after investigating why burrs kept sticking to his clothing during a hike.

When we allow ourselves to see idea generation as innate or random—as something people are either born with or gifted by some other entity without warning—we take our own agency out of the creative process. We're telling ourselves we just don't have "it" or that we have to keep waiting for our "big idea" to come to us, when it's ready... when the muse permits... someday... if it ever happens.

But the reality is, *anyone* can generate content ideas quickly and easily, if they have the right framework. And that is what I will offer you in this book: my very own time-tested framework for thinking of content ideas—100 or more content ideas at a time, in fact—and a handy list of subcategories that you can use to guide your brainstorms, no matter what type of content you need to create.

This framework is the codification of a process I have used myself for more than 15 years, generating hundreds of thousands of unique content ideas for nearly endless platforms and purposes. I used this framework to fill the pages of all those school publications I worked for. I used it to present fresh ideas to the hundreds of brands requesting content campaigns when I worked as the first editor of branded content at the *New York Times*. I used it to maintain a pace of six articles per month when I had a column on Inc.com. I've used it to populate personal blogs, company YouTube profiles, startup marketing plans, and more with engaging original content.

But this framework isn't one that works only for me.

I've helped thousands of people adopt this framework as their own in workshops, through conference keynotes, and during employee training sessions. I've watched marketers, sales professionals, engineers, startup founders, entrepreneurs, students, and other individuals skeptically enter a ballroom or conference room, and leave an hour later with a notebook full of content ideas and a new perspective on their own creativity.

My hope is that if you read this book, start to finish, the same can happen for you. By the time you finish this book, you too will have a notebook full of new content ideas, and a newfound confidence in your ability to conjure up new strategic ideas quickly and easily. By the time we're done, coming up with 100 content ideas will seem like a walk in the park.

• •

Did You Know?

There's also a companion workbook for The Content Fuel Framework, which will guide you through the process of generating hundreds of content ideas. Head to www.contentfuelframework .com/workbook to learn more and order yours.

• •

Content Fuel

As a **consultant,** advisor, and trainer, I've worked with all kinds of companies—from global tech giants and national insurance companies to mobile sports startups and local diamond retailers. In my workshops and executive coaching sessions, I often ask the question "How long would it take you to come up with 100 content ideas for your brand or company?"

So often, the answer is: "I can't."

When I dig deeper into this answer, I find that many of the people who feel this way share the same fears:

Where are the ideas going to come from?
What if I can't think of anything new to say?
What if I'm just not creative enough?

My guess is, if you're picking up this book, you've had some version of these thoughts yourself. You're not alone.

But before you decide that coming up with 100 content ideas is out of reach, think instead about your confidence in your ability to come up with a list of 100 cities, or 100 living things, or 100 first names. If you were tasked with creating any one of these lists, you'd undoubtedly create a plan of attack, however subconsciously, by thinking about specific sub-groups within the category that would help guide your thinking.

For cities, you might start by naming all the municipalities where you've lived, followed by nearby cities you've seen on the local news, and any you've passed on the interstate. If you're a sports fan, you might find yourself listing the cities with NFL teams, then NBA teams, MLB teams, and NHL teams. If you're a frequent traveler, you might list major cities with airports. If you decided to start by naming all 50 state capitals, you'd find yourself halfway to 100 already.

If you had to name 100 living things, you might start with animals that are common as pets, then move on to animals that are native to your home, then list more exotic animals you typically see in a zoo. You might also choose to create your list by region or ecosystem, first listing ocean creatures, then rainforest creatures, then desert creatures, and so on.

If the task were to list 100 first names, you'd likely start by listing your own first and middle names, then those of your family and your close friends. Once you'd run through those individuals, you'd move on to other groups, such as past and present neighbors, coworkers, and classmates. Depending on your interests, you might also use a category like musicians, actors, athletes, Broadway stars, or politicians to guide your thinking.

For any type of list, using an alphabetical approach might also give you a great framework—you might list cities from

Anchorage to Yuka, creatures from aardvark to zebra, or names from Aaron to Zeke. You might also try to create your list in order of size (be it population, weight, or number of letters), or something else entirely.

Truthfully, it doesn't matter which framework you use so much as it matters—simply—that you have one. Frameworks like these act as guardrails for your brain, giving you a place to start and a direction in which to move with confidence.

The problem, when it comes to the task of generating content ideas, is that most of us lack a framework for how to think about them. We don't have ready subcategories that guide our thinking and allow us to generate lists of new ideas quickly and efficiently.

The secret lies in knowing that a content idea is truly just the combination of two elements: a focus and a format.

Content Idea =
Focus + Format

Focus

Your content focus is the "point of concentration." Your focus is what you are examining, discussing, illuminating, sharing, or conveying.

For our purposes as content creators and storytellers, the focus of our content is our message, and the approach we take to sharing it.

For example, a piece of content might put the spotlight on a person, such as the founder of a company, someone who has inspired you, a well-known figure in an industry, or a customer who has an interesting story to tell. The content might share information about their life, their experience, their background, their perspective, their favorite things, their family, or other relevant personal details. We'd call this kind of content, with one or more individuals as the focus, a people-focused piece of content.

Or, you may want to create a piece of content that looks back at the past, such as the story of how a company was founded, the milestones in the development of a product or industry, the events throughout time that contributed to a present-day situation, or the evolution of something over time. This content might share stories from important dates in the past, archival photos of people and places, quotes from historical documents like diaries or maps, and other information about past events. A piece of content that looks back in this way is history-focused.

Along with People and History, other focuses that I have found useful for content creation include Basics, Details, Process, Curation, Data, Product, Example, and Opinion. In the next few chapters, we'll explore each of these 10 Focuses more deeply, and you'll learn how you can apply them to create your own original content.

Format

In its most general sense, the word *format* refers to the shape, size, and makeup of something, the way it's organized, or what it's made from.

For our purposes as content creators and brand storytellers, the format is the way that a piece of content is brought to life: the form it takes when it leaves your brain and enters the world, and the means by which our audience can engage with or consume it.

In addition to the 10 Focuses, I have 10 Formats that I like to use when brainstorming content ideas: Writing, Infographic, Audio, Video, Live Video, Image Gallery, Timeline, Quiz, Tool, and Map. Each has its own best use.

For example, if you wanted to create a lengthy and important conversation or interview with someone of influence, you could write out the entire exchange, word for word, and share it in written format. But if you wanted to make sure your audience hears the tone of voice used and feels the impact of every pause, laugh, and hesitation, you could record that conversation and share it in audio form.

Let's say you want to create a piece of content that coaches your audience through the process of replacing the serpentine belt on a particular type of car. A piece of writing alone might not provide enough detail for your audience. You'd probably want to include some visuals, to make sure your audience can see each of the actions you take and hear you explain what you're doing each step of the way. This piece of content would probably be most useful if it were presented as a video.

In the latter half of this book, we'll explore all 10 Formats (and more) in detail, sharing more information about how to create content that will be presented through each of them. But it's worth noting that many of the pieces of content we create and encounter are presented in more than one format: written pieces, for example, are almost always accompanied by videos, infographics, or maps, and timelines tend to be populated with snippets of writing, audio, or images. These combinations of formats create multimedia pieces that tell richer stories and satisfy our audience's expectations for more engaging and dynamic content experiences.*

---

* Multimedia content is also favored or prioritized by many of the algorithms that govern social and search discovery.

The framework presented in this book will help you meet this growing appetite for multimedia by encouraging you to explore the multiple ways in which you can present every story you want to tell. Use this framework in your content planning, and it will soon become second nature to consider alternative storytelling formats that might complement your primary format choice.

Almost any piece of content you have ever created or consumed can be interpreted through this framework: all of them have a focus and a format.

Consider *Serial*, the investigative podcast phenomenon that took the world by storm in 2014. Season one of the hit show dug into the trial and questionable conviction of 18-year-old Adnan Syed for the murder of his former girl-friend, Hae Min Lee, in Baltimore, Maryland. The riveting story spent weeks atop the iTunes podcast charts. Without a doubt, *Serial* was a cultural sensation. The podcast focuses on history—of the case, of the trial, of Adnan, and of other key figures—and it's told through the format of audio.

Focus = History
Format = Audio

Or perhaps you recall a quiz from the *New York Times* that got a lot of attention in 2013, called "How Y'all, Youse and You Guys Talk."* The quiz contained 25 multiple-choice

---

* You can read more about this quiz at by entering the title in the search fields at www.towardsdatascience.com.

questions asking respondents what they call common items and situations; the answers resulted in a custom map of the United States that identified, with shocking accuracy, areas where the respondent was raised, lived, or spent significant time. The data that informed these questions and the mapped results were all drawn from a Harvard linguistics study. This content focused on data, and was presented in the form of a quiz first, and a map second.

$$Focus = Data$$
$$Format = Quiz + Map$$

Focus Before Format

We know that a content idea is made up of these two things: a focus, and a format.

But here's the key: it's not simply that you need one of each—a focus and a format—to create a complete content idea. The order in which you select these two elements is important, too.

Always start with the focus, and *then* determine which format is best suited to the story that you want to tell.

As storytellers, once we have a focus in mind, we can ask ourselves "What is the best way to bring this story to life?"

But the instinct is often to do the opposite: to start our content brainstorms with the format, simply because the format is the more visible and familiar aspect of content ideas. We already have a shared language, as content consumers, about the nature of writing or video, for example. But having a conversation about the merits of "people-focused content" or "product-focused content" may come less naturally.

When we start with a format instead of a focus, we are assuming that *how we say something* is more important than *what we say*. And that is simply not true.

These "format-first" brainstorms are all too common, for corporate content marketers and independent brand storytellers alike. So often, brainstorms or pitch meetings are called to order with a format already chosen, forcing us to come up with a "video idea" or an "infographic idea" or an "article idea," simply because an executive requested or suggested a particular format or because there's pressure to post content on a particular platform.

Such brainstorms almost always lead to content ideas where the focus and the format are mismatched. By forcing stories to be told in formats that don't suit the narrative or the audience, we not only rob our ideas of their potential, we also rob our audience of the value these stories could have provided.

Let's say your founder has a fascinating background and history. If you walked into that brainstorm having already decided that you need "a video idea," then you might end up creating a mind-numbingly boring video, where your founder sits in front of a white background, stares straight into the camera for 30 minutes, and shares their entire life story in chronological order. While this is technically "a video idea," it certainly isn't the most engaging way to share your founder's story—meaning it's not a video that most of us would want to watch.

But if you follow the proper order for content idea generation—choosing a focus, and *then* choosing a format—you could ask yourself "What's the best way to bring our founder's story to life?" Knowing your founder is not so comfortable on video and that their backstory is quite long, you might have chosen to create an interactive timeline, with photos and audio snippets platted along the way to make that long story fresh and exciting for the audience to explore.

When we choose the focus before the format, we are letting our stories unfold and be told in the most natural way, which ultimately serves both our stories and our audience better.

Introducing the Content Fuel Framework

In the chapters to come, we're going to explore and explain some common (and not-so-common) content focuses and content formats, in the hopes that you have more inspiration to draw from and more options to consider when entering into future content brainstorms.

But understanding the main 10 Focuses and 10 Formats is just the start: for many of the creators, producers, and strategists that I've worked with during consulting, conference workshops, and corporate training, simply having a list of these options isn't quite enough to make brainstorms easier, more strategic, or more productive.

To help make this list of options more useful and actionable, I created the Content Fuel Framework. Simply put, this is a matrix, or grid, built from the 10 Focuses and the 10 Formats, visually creating space for 100 new focus/format combinations, and 100 ways to tell any story.

The purpose of the Content Fuel Framework isn't to force you to actually create or execute on a piece of content at every single one of the 100 focus/format intersections, but instead to challenge you to think in new content combinations and to explore new possibilities for the way you tell stories.

Content Fuel Framework

	People	Basics	Details	History
Writing				
Infographic				
Audio				
Video				
Live Video				
Image Gallery				
Timeline				
Quiz				
Tool				
Map				

FOCUS × FORMAT

Process	Curation	Data	Product	Example	Opinion

In a workshop or training scenario, I often use the grid as a game board, of sorts. I arrange participants into small groups, and give each group a pair of 10-sided dice: the 10 numbers on the black die correspond to the 10 possible options for content focus, and 10 numbers on the red die represent the 10 options for content format. I ask them to roll the dice, creating a completely random focus/format combination, and to spend a few minutes brainstorming what content they could bring to life with that combination.

Overwhelmingly, the feedback on this exercise is that it created entirely new ways of thinking about their products, messaging, and stories, and encouraged them to present stories in entirely new ways that they had never considered.

Sometimes, just one or two of the 100+ ideas that participants come up with are ultimately produced after our workshop ends. That's OK. After all, we all have limitations on our time, budget, and other resources. As much as we might like to, few of us get to spend all day producing innovative new content pieces in exciting new ways.

To that point, the Content Fuel Framework wasn't designed to be a mandatory 100-idea checklist. (I know that it's neither wise nor fun to spend your time thinking up amazing new content ideas that you know may never come to life.*) Instead, it's designed to encourage you to think about content in new ways, to facilitate the process of rapid content idea generation, and to allow you to pick the best of the best from the list that you ultimately generate.

---

*   This is the content strategy equivalent of test-driving cars or trying on wedding dresses outside of your budget. It feels great at the moment, but leads to a lot of disappointment.

How to Make the Content Fuel System Work for You

This Content Fuel Framework is a 10-by-10 matrix, featuring all 10 Focuses and all 10 Formats explored in this book. These are the focuses and formats that I find to be the most frequently used among the marketers and creators I work with. But the arrangement I propose and the focuses and formats I choose are absolutely not the "one true framework" for content idea generation.

My hope is that you can use this book to learn more about the potential of the content formats and focuses you frequently use, discover some content focuses and formats you may not have considered, and assemble a version of the Content Fuel Framework that's right for you.

Here are some of the ways you can customize this system to ensure it serves your unique content needs, and that it takes your own resources and preferences into account.

Explore: My recommendation for this book is to read it through, from start to finish. You may find that some of the content focuses and formats we explore are more familiar to you, while others are new and require a little more of your time and consideration. That's OK. The goal here is to help you understand your many options—both the known and the new—so you can make more strategic and creative content choices in the future.

Select: After you've read through the 10 Focus chapters and 10 Format chapters, you should have a fairly good idea of which options are feasible given your resources, as well as which will be most interesting for you to explore. I want to encourage you to stretch yourself: don't just use the ones that seem familiar and safe, but also use some that are new or challenging. That's where your exciting new content ideas are hiding.

Adapt: Using all 10 Focuses and all 10 Formats in the Content Fuel Framework creates a 10 by 10 grid, but you can choose to expand this matrix or shrink it for your purposes, based on which focuses and formats you want to brainstorm around. You can make your grid with eight focuses and nine formats, or seven focuses and 13 formats, or 16 focuses and just three formats. The math is up to you. Keep in mind, however, that the more focuses and formats you include on each axis, the more potential ideas you can generate from a single brainstorm. To make the exercise productive, I would advise making sure that the grid you ultimately settle on still gives you 25 or more ideas.

Multiply: We'll talk more about this starting on page 163, but there are also easy ways to create multiple variations on a single content idea, allowing you to turn one initial idea into three, five, or even 10 unique versions of that original idea. As you're building your own grid, don't forget to create a reference list of the examples we'll discuss in the Multipliers chapter that make the most sense for you, so you can turn each great idea into several.

The Work Before the Work

Like any endeavor in business (or in life, really) you should have some sort of mission in mind before you get started. All the great brainstorming in the world won't get you far if you're not sure why you're brainstorming content ideas in the first place.

Unfortunately, I can't tell you exactly why you should create content. But I can share some of the common reasons why people do, in the hopes that one or more might resonate with you and help guide you toward finding your purpose.

For many people, content creation is a job function. If you work on the marketing or communications team for a company, educational institution, or non-profit, for example, then content creation and distribution may be one tactic you use to achieve the broader organizational goals set by a team of executives.

Your content may be created with the intention of selling more products, enrolling more students, securing more donations, increasing customer loyalty, or educating potential customers.

For others, content creation is a tool for building reputation and reach. If you're a speaker, author, consultant, influencer, creator, artist, freelancer, or some other type of entrepreneur, then your content creation and distribution is likely a way to build a personal and professional brand.

The content you create may be used for showcasing your expertise and talents, building fan loyalty, earning press coverage, attracting paying opportunities, and retaining an engaged fan base to support your projects, and potentially your products, too.

But content creation can serve other purposes. If you're creatively inclined, perhaps your blog, YouTube channel, online comic, or your dog's Instagram account offers you a creative outlet to share your thoughts and use your talents. You may not be worried about monetizing, and you just like having a space to create.

If you're driven by activism, you may like using your blog or social presence to further a cause close to your heart, promoting behavior change and habit adoption, or encouraging support for organizations you care about. You're less concerned with profit than with the opportunity to use content to create change.

Before diving into the chapters that follow, take a few moments to answer the questions on page 23 and 24, to help better understand the reasons why you need or want to create content, whether they're similar to what's listed here, or other reasons entirely.

Spend some time writing out your answers to these prompts, and examining the results—this should help you determine *your* reasons for creating content. Fundamentally, though, any of the reasons you come up with will require you to tackle the same challenge: to communicate your message in a way that engages your current audience, attracts a new audience, and expands your impact on the world. Stories allow us to do that, and the Content Fuel Framework gives you the ability to consistently generate new story ideas, so you can achieve your content goals, whatever they may be.

Let's dive in.

**Here are some prompts you can use
to get clarity on your content purpose:**

I create content because . . .

_____

_____

_____

The primary audience that I create content for is . . .

_____

_____

_____

Ideally, if my audience consumes my content, it would lead to . . .

_____

_____

_____

I hope that my audience will describe my content as . . .

_____

_____

_____

I hope that my audience will say my content makes them feel . . .

_____

_____

_____

I would like to create content similar to the content I see from . . .

_____

_____

_____

I hope that creating content will make me feel . . .

_____

_____

_____

THE
10
FOCUSES

1

People

CONTENT FOCUSED on people is content that tells the story of a person or a group of individuals. In journalism, we'd call this type of people-focused content a profile or feature.

Profiles provide details about an individual, offering insights into their personality, perspective, character, background, achievements, behaviors, attitudes, beliefs, preferences, influences, style, and other aspects of their life.

Most often, these types of stories focus on newsworthy individuals, such that the audience would be interested enough in their story to invest the time into learning more about them. Well-known individuals—musicians, actors, athletes, politicians, and other public figures—often have that level of audience interest built in, given their influence, reputation, and existing fan base.

But lesser-known individuals and everyday people may earn a level of interest through their experiences, achievements, participation in newsworthy events, or other unique and noteworthy actions.* When cameras capture everyday people committing crimes, doing good deeds, or managing exceptional feats and the footage inspires widespread public curiosity about the individual behind the acts, this is that phenomenon at work.

People-focused content generally includes direct input from the person being profiled, in the form of interviews, quotes, or other types of participation. These stories also tend to include input from others who know the subject well: family, friends, coworkers, or neighbors, for example. Including the subject's own input, as well as the input of those who know them well, paints a more complete picture of the person being featured.

And while most profiles focus on an individual person, it's possible to create this same type of people-focused content about a closely connected group of people: a family, team, club, department, class, or other tight-knit community.

The instinct with people-focused content—particularly for content created by a company—is to remain tightly focused on the people inside the organization. But telling stories about others—customers, community partners, neighbors, vendors— allows organizations to shine the spotlight on all of the people who impact the organization and demonstrate its values.

When the focus of these content pieces is on someone noteworthy, their name is generally included in the headline or title of the piece. When the individual may not be known or recognized by name, their achievement or relevance may

---

* See Jimmy Breslin's 1963 profile of Clifton Pollard, the man who dug President John F. Kennedy's grave at Arlington. Breslin was known for unique profiles like this, earning a Pulitzer Prize in 1986 "for columns which consistently champion ordinary citizens."

be noted in the headline instead. Here's how these people-focused headlines might look:

- **Name:** A Candidate on a Mission
- How **Name** Is Changing the Film Industry
- Meet the **Chef** Behind This Year's Biggest Food Trend
- **"Quote"**: The Unlikely Hero **Who** Stopped a Robbery

Examples of People-Focused Content

Many times, the goal of people-focused content is to profile the prominent, or to share more intimate details about someone with whom the audience is already familiar. In these cases, the goal and challenge is to obtain new information the audience doesn't already know about the subject.

- A fashion blogger may profile a well-known designer to see how his recent move to Asia has influenced his work, in hopes of sharing new insights into his process.

- A tech company may publish a lengthy interview with their outgoing CEO, unearthing new stories and learnings from her tenure at the company and sharing new details about her next chapter.

Sometimes, people-focused content takes an almost opposite approach, by attempting to shine a spotlight on the unknown. In these cases, the goal is often to introduce the audience to someone they don't yet know, but would likely be interested in learning more about.

- A non-profit might create a written profile of a person who has benefited from their programming, assistance, or fundraising, helping underscore the impact of the organization's work by showing how it has directly affected the life of one individual.

- A sports franchise might create a video in which they follow their stadium groundskeepers for a day to show all the work that goes into keeping the facilities clean, safe, and ready for regular competition, giving fans a new appreciation for the non-athlete members of the team.

Here are some individuals that may be good subjects for people-focused content:

- **Major Players**: C-suite members, officials, executives, leaders, decision makers, candidates, celebrities, thought leaders
- **Main Players**: employees, staff, faculty, students, workers, crew
- **Supporters/Partners**: customers, clients, members, subscribers, fans, users, attendees, participants, vendors, providers, sponsors, advertisers, donors, benefactors
- **Exceptional**: winners, record holders, finalists, firsts, heroes, honorees
- **Past**: outgoing, ousted, alumni, formers, elders, retired
- **Future**: new, next, incoming, rising stars, prospective
- **Others**: unknowns, neighbors, competitors, creators, inventors, opposition, charities

. . . .

Questions to Consider
When Creating People-Focused Content

▸ What people might the audience be already interested in learning more about?

▸ What people should the audience know more about, even if they aren't asking?

  Which people contribute to this story, but haven't been given attention before?

▸ What research could be done about the subject in advance to avoid basic questions?

▸ What unique perspective could be taken for a story on this person?

  What can be uncovered about the person that hasn't been said before?

  What questions will the person be unlikely to have heard before?

▸ Who knows this person well enough to offer additional insights about them?

▸ Which exact quotes from this person are compelling enough to be included as is, and which would be better paraphrased?

. . . .

VISIT www.contentfuelframework.com/focuses and click "People" for a list of additional tools and resources for creating people-focused content.

2

Basics

CONTENT THAT focuses on the basics attempts to provide a general overview of a subject, offering definitions, background information, relevant context, and references for additional information.

Content about the basics can be thought of as "101" content, or content that assumes little to no prior knowledge of a subject, and attempts to help the audience understand the subject better. Given that its purpose is to provide introductory information, content that focuses on basic information is generally presented in a clear and concise way to help the audience consume it quickly and easily.

Oftentimes, basics-focused content is intended to provide an approachable explanation of an otherwise complicated subject. Other content of this type centers on subjects that entered the public conversation or awareness rather suddenly: current events, pop culture references, slang terms, emerging technology, rising stars, rapidly growing companies.

Basics-focused content is often easy to recognize because the headline or title structure tends to acknowledge its role, so that a beginner audience will know that the content was created for them. Content that focuses on the basics often carries a headline or title like this:

- **A Beginner's Guide** to Bitcoin
- Moving to New York: **The Basics**
- **What You Need to Know** Before Adopting a Shelter Dog
- **What's the Deal** with Vaping?
- Mortgages **101**

This type of content can often form the foundation of a content strategy, by covering all of the key terms, trends, people, and more in an industry or niche. It might not be the most differentiated content, as many other content producers will likely be looking to create a similar foundation if they share the same industry or niche. But offering this type of content ensures that someone who wants to learn about this subject won't have to look to your competitors for information.

For that reason, it's a good idea to have a large list of potential ideas for basics-focused content, and to work on building this base of content in the background of more timely content activities. These pieces make great assignments for new writers and can also be great filler content during times when resources aren't available to create more involved content.

Examples of Basics-Focused Content

Much basics-focused content is intended to serve as a cheat sheet for a complicated subject, such that someone can achieve a basic level of understanding or conversational fluency on a subject without having to spend significant time or effort researching it themselves.

- A physicist might write a brief article on her blog titled "What Exactly Is the Higgs Boson?" explaining the origins, naming, and other basic details about this subatomic particle.

- A brand sponsoring a major sporting event might create a two-minute video explaining the basic rules of the game, along with some key terms and other context, to help those who are less familiar with the game enjoy the celebration.

Similarly, trend briefings can provide a basic overview of an emerging topic, helping the audience feel informed about a subject that is quickly becoming important or relevant. These content pieces serve much the same function as a cheat sheet might, but often come about more quickly, in response to something that suddenly gained public attention.

- A chef or food blogger might write a short blog post titled "What's the Deal with CBD in Food?" to help their audience understand the marijuana-derived ingredient they're likely seeing popping up in their local stores, restaurants, and cafes, or in the news.

- A marketing thought leader might create a video on YouTube called "3 Things You Need to Know about Facebook's Latest Algorithm Update" to help their followers understand

the basics of the most recent changes to the social network's
newsfeed.*

Some content focuses on the basics by providing simple detail
about several key elements within a given subject, whether
those are individuals, terms, or other influences. These content
pieces are often structured as lists, or broken up into sections.

· A coffee shop might create a small illustrated guide with the
title "Cafe Vocabulary Basics" to explain the most common
drink items and terms customers will find on cafe menus, helping them feel more comfortable and informed when ordering.

· A jeweler might create a brief article that explains the impor-
tance of a diamond's cut, and offers clear descriptions of five
common cuts to help customers understand how to evaluate,
select, and shop for a properly cut diamond.

---

* Bonus: they'd get to make a new version of this video whenever the algorithm is updated.

· ·

Questions to Consider
When Creating Basics-Focused Content

▶ What basic information might the audience need to know more about?

▶ If someone encountered this topic for the first time, what would they need to know?

▶ What terms, people, places, items, and more might be confusing for them?

▶ What does the audience need to understand for them to become informed customers?

▶ What emerging trends might the audience need more context for?

▶ What questions does the audience ask that can be answered?

What audience questions can be discovered through keyword research?

What audience questions can be discovered through social media?

What common questions does the audience ask sales, customer service, etc.?

· ·

VISIT www.contentfuelframework.com/focuses and click "Basics" for a list of helpful tools and additional resources about basics-focused content.

FOCUS

3

Details

WHEN CONTENT focuses on the details, it aims to provide a lengthy, comprehensive, or otherwise in-depth look at a particular subject.

Details-focused content is the more thorough iteration of the basics-focused content discussed in the previous chapter. Where basics-focused content might provide introductory information on a topic, details-focused content assumes the audience already has a basic level of understanding, and aims to deepen that understanding by providing significantly more detailed information.

Journalists might call this type of content in-depth or long-form, meaning the content is providing a lot of information and may require more than the average amount of words, print space, or playing time in order to achieve the necessary level of depth and detail.

As with basics-focused content, content pieces that focus on the details can often be identified by the structure of their headlines and titles, which tend to acknowledge the audience's presumed level of knowledge about the subject. In-depth content headlines typically look like this:

- **An Expert's Guide** to Blockchain
- The Electoral College: **An Advanced Guide**
- **Everything You Need to Know** About Buying a Home
- **A Complete History** of Space Exploration
- **How to** Prep for a Race **like a Pro/Expert/Ultra-Marathoner/ Olympian**

Basics-focused content often serves as a reference, providing significant educational value for the audience, attracting new audiences over time, and being returned to time and again. For this reason, it's often wise (and even necessary) to revise and update this type of content to ensure it stays relevant and accurate as new information, research, or developments emerge on the subject.

Details-focused content often takes longer to create, as it may require significant research and time to compile the necessary amount of relevant details. Since creating content of this type requires time and other resources, it serves as a great choice for monthly, quarterly, or annual content pieces that can be used as an anchor for more frequent pieces with other focuses.

While it's not impossible to find examples of detail-focused pieces about emerging trends, this isn't as common, since trends may rise and fall in popularity before a detailed content piece can be properly researched, published, and shared.

Examples of Details-Focused Content

The depth of a details-focused piece is often best understood in contrast to its basics-focused counterpart. To that end, the examples below have been drawn from the chapter on Focus 2: Basics, and adapted to reflect the more thorough, comprehensive approach one would expect with a details-focused content piece.

In the previous chapter, we discussed how basics-focused content can be presented as a cheat sheet to distill complicated subjects into quick-reference content. But when content is focused on providing details, it takes a more complete guide approach. In the case of this type of content, the goal is to serve as a one-stop shop for all the relevant information on a given subject.

- A physicist might write an in-depth article for her blog titled "A Complete History of the Higgs Boson." The piece would explain in great detail the particle's significance, detail the various attempts to confirm its existence, and summarize the work and life of the individuals who contributed to its discovery, and may reference recent literature on the subject to help the audience continue their detailed exploration of it.

- A brand sponsoring a major sporting event might create a 10-minute video as a way to engage superfans. The video would give a detailed history of the event, share archival footage, offer facts about the venue, introduce all the major teams and players in the game, and give an in-depth review of relevant data, projections, analysis, and commentary about the upcoming event.

As we discussed, trend briefings tend to be less common for details-focused content, because the level of detail they require can inhibit their ability to be put out in a timely fashion. That being said, trends can be examined in a detailed way through trend reviews, which allow for more significant exploration of a trend, either after its peak or after it has proven its staying power.

- A chef or food blogger might write an in-depth article titled "CBD-Infused Food: Examining the Science, Reception, and Regulation" to provide a more thorough analysis and exploration of the science behind the marijuana-derived ingredient, the benefits and risks associated with its use, the relevant regulation around its sale, and additional details that particularly conscious and curious consumers would want to know.

- A marketing thought leader might create a 15-minute YouTube video called "Everything You Need to Know About Facebook's Latest Algorithm Update," sharing the results of a two-week test they ran to confirm the significance of the changes, offering a detailed analysis of available recourse for those impacted, and comparing this update to some of the previous updates.

While basics-focused content might examine only the key elements of a particular issue, a details-focused piece would take a more thorough approach, in an attempt to create a more in-depth report on a particular subject, covering more than just the most basic or important elements.

- A coffee shop might create a piece called "How to Make Coffee like a Barista," offering a detailed explanation about every part of the coffee preparation process: identifying different roasts, grinding beans, brewing by different means, operating espresso machine equipment, learning different drink recipes, and more.*

---

* I'm a coffee person, so prepare yourself: this won't be the last reference to coffee in this book!

- A jeweler might create an in-depth piece of content explaining the 4 Cs of diamonds—Carat, Cut, Color, and Clarity—to help more discerning shoppers learn everything about diamond quality, including how each of these factors are measured, the scales used for measurement, who certifies the stones, how each factor impacts the price of the stone, and other considerations that may come up in a discussion of a stone's quality and cost.

· ·

Questions to Consider
When Creating Details-Focused Content

- Is there a piece of existing basics-focused content that can be expanded?

- How advanced is the audience for this content piece?

- What would an advanced audience want to know more about for this topic?

- How much detail is necessary for the audience's level of understanding?

- What research could be used to add credible details to this content?

- Which expert perspectives or additional sources will add credibility to this piece?

- How long will it take to create a significantly detailed content piece?

▶ Could a complementary basics-focused piece pair easily with this piece?

▶ How might the content be organized to make it approachable, despite its depth or length?

. . . .

VISIT www.contentfuelframework.com/focuses and click "Details" for a list of helpful tools and additional resources about details-focused content.

4

History

CONTENT FOCUSED on history aims to provide relevant information from the past about a particular topic, whether it's an object, event, product, industry, person, organization, or something else.

Focusing on history for a piece of content requires looking back into the past, oftentimes further back than the content creator may have been able to experience or remember. For this reason, history-focused content generally requires a bit more time, research, and outside sources than some of the other content focuses in order to be complete and accurate.

Historical content generally has a long shelf life; because it addresses something that has already happened, the content rarely needs to be revised or changed, beyond potentially having new information added. As such, a single, well-researched piece of historical content can serve as a resource and provide value to the audience for a long time after it's completed.

It's also important to note that historical content does not need to focus strictly on *your own* history. In fact, it probably shouldn't. Exploring the history of subjects that fall outside of your own experience or offerings is more interesting to research and more interesting for your audience to engage with.

Creating history-focused content gives you the opportunity to explore many areas: industry, product category, specific product, technology, event, individual, organization, group, geographic area, structure, landmark, tradition, behavior, habit, belief, trend, word, and more.

Content pieces that focus on history can often be identified by the structure of their headlines and titles, which allude to looking back through time. Historical content might have a headline or title like this:

- **The History** of Shapewear
- **Looking Back** on 100+ Years of Film
- Autonomous Vehicles: **How We Got Here***
- **The Evolution** of Refrigeration

Examples of History-Focused Content

A common type of historical content is the origin story, sharing the history of an organization or executive. These tend to live on the static pages of a website, like "About Me" or "Our History," and provide a snapshot of past events that informed the individual or organization.

---

* "How we got here" has a fun double meaning for a story about autonomous vehicles, but works for retrospectives about subjects without wheels, too.

- A family owned farm may have a "History" tab on their website that shares the details of the farm and what it has produced throughout the last five generations, complete with family photos, old posters from the farmer's market, and a family tree.

- An entrepreneur may have an "About" page on their personal website that shares relevant details of their childhood and education, along with the previous work experience that led them to start their current venture.

The more dynamic version of an origin story is an evolution piece or trends piece, which aims to track change or progress on a particular subject before the present date. This type of story tends to live as a content piece, as opposed to being a section of a static web page.

- A tech blog might create a lengthy written piece explaining the creation and evolution of cryptocurrency—from the first use of the word to the present day—offering insights into how and when the various types of cryptocurrency rose in popularity, how markets have responded, how regulation has changed, and how public opinion has shifted.

- A politician might create a blog post in support of an upcoming piece of legislation, sharing the history of the issue it addresses, how the need has evolved over time, and how previous legislation and politicians have failed to address it properly in the past.

· ·

Questions to Consider
When Creating History-Focused Content

- Does this particular subject or topic have a rich history that could be explored?

  Has the prevalence, perception, or other aspects of this subject changed over time?

- How far back should this content go to provide all the relevant historical context?

- Is special research necessary to find accurate historical information and content assets?

  Do special rights need to be secured for use of these content assets?

- What qualified individuals are knowledgeable on the history of this subject and could add value by providing expert information, clarification, confirmation, or other context?

- Are there libraries, historical societies, or other organizations and resources that would be helpful for compiling and finding these historical resources?

- Has examining the history of this subject uncovered additional stories that can be told?

· ·

VISIT www.contentfuelframework.com/focuses and click "History" for a list of helpful tools and additional resources about history-focused content.

5

Process

ONTENT THAT focuses on a process is designed to help the audience understand how something happens and, sometimes, help them replicate that process themselves.

Most often, process-focused content is instructional, and is presented as a set of ordered steps, with the goal of helping the audience complete a process. This type of content can focus on a wide variety of processes someone may have to complete: fixing, creating, starting, stopping, increasing, decreasing, selecting, adapting, editing, adjusting, replacing, updating, installing, setting up, and more.

Such content might focus on physical processes, like replacing a part inside a laptop or making a quilt out of old t-shirts. But it could also focus on less tangible processes, like dealing with grief, picking a college major, or determining why a baby is crying.

Other times, process-focused content may simply describe or share a process that is *not* intended to be replicated by the audience consuming that content. This type of content typically shares behind-the-scenes information about a process that the audience may be curious about but may not otherwise get to see.

A great example of this is the Discovery Channel show *How It's Made*. Each 30-minute television episode features four different factory montages, walking viewers through how four different products are made.* In season three, episode six, viewers learned the steps it takes to make yogurt, candles, neon signs, and book bindings. In season 25, episode 10, the show explains the processes used to create mountain bike suspensions, surgical sutures, grain dryers, and frying pans.

It's unlikely that viewers tune into the show with the intention of using the five-minute video montage and voiceover to create their own neon sign or grain dryer—assuming they happen to have the raw materials, machines, tools, certifications, and experience to do so. Instead, the show simply offers a sneak peek into a factory, facility, industry, and process viewers might never otherwise get to see, allowing them to feel smarter and more informed for having seen it.

Whether your process-focused content is intended to be instructional or informational, it's almost always educational, teaching the audience about a process they did not previously know about or understand.

The headlines and titles of process-focused content also tend to have some commonalities, like so:

---

* Fun fact: There have been 400+ episodes of How It's Made since the show debuted. With four products featured per episode, Discovery Channel has shown how 1,600+ objects get made!

- **How to** Start Your Own YouTube Channel
- Creating a Custom Closet with Ikea Hacks, **Step by Step**
- **What It Takes** to Become a Pilot
- **How** Computers Get **Made/Fixed/Shipped/Updated**
- **Behind the Scenes** of a Paris Fashion Show

A note: regardless of whether your intent is to inform or to instruct, it's important to consider the ramifications of providing detailed information about processes that—if replicated—may bring harm to the audience or others. Exploring processes related to criminal activities, self-harm, weapons creation, and other dangerous behaviors may not only educate your audience, but also unwittingly enable or encourage bad actors to complete these processes. Before creating content that focuses on potentially dangerous processes, always pause to reflect on whether the educational value significantly outweighs the risk of harm, and how you might further mitigate the risk of harm.

Examples of Process-Focused Content

Most process-focused content is instructional content, where the steps being shared are designed to be followed. Because the content is meant to serve as a guide for a process, it's often very detailed, and includes multiple content formats—writing, diagrams, photos, and more—to help aid in the completion of the described process.

- A marketing consultant might create step-by-step written instructions for setting up a simple Facebook advertising campaign.

- A plumber might make a video showing how to stop a toilet from running, so the audience can follow along, opening the tank and making adjustments to the parts inside.

Within the category of instructional content, there are also plenty of recipes, where a list of ingredients, measurements, and instructions for combination are shared. The goal with recipes is for the audience to follow the steps to make something.*

Most often, recipes are for things the audience can eat or drink, like breakfasts, lunches, dinners, snacks, cocktails, smoothies, or desserts. Occasionally, though, "recipe" is also used for cooking or mixing processes where the final product is non-edible, as is the case with recipes for making homemade cleaning supplies, beauty products, and some crafts.

- A food blogger might create a photo slideshow sharing the ingredients, measurements, instructions, and visuals for each step to make her famous gluten-free banana bread.

- A researcher, speaker, and author who focuses on going green and reducing waste might share a written recipe for all-natural glass cleaner to use around the home.

Process-focused content can also go behind-the-scenes, where the audience gets to see a process without any intention of replicating it themselves.

- An athlete might create a series of diary-like videos showing what it's like to travel with them, train with them, and otherwise prepare for the big game, taking fans into their process and world in a way that can't be seen from the outside.

- An academic institution might create a written guide that shares how they evaluate applications, walking through the criteria they consider, the materials they review, and the questions they ask, helping prospective students and parents better understand the admissions process.

---

* While most recipes are intended to be instructional, most of us watch recipe videos on social media without any intention of making them, rendering them informational.

Questions to Consider
When Creating Process-Focused Content

▶ For which processes does the audience need advice, guidance, or help?

Can more information about these processes be shared in a way that's helpful?

▶ Is this content intended to be instructional or informational?

▶ Is there already significant content providing instruction on this process?

Can a different perspective, approach, or adaptation of this process be provided?

▶ What expertise is necessary to teach this process?

Can this expertise be found internally, or are outside experts necessary?

▶ How detailed should the content be in the description of each step?

Has enough detail been provided to allow the audience to replicate each step properly, if needed?

▶ Are there any legal, ethical, or moral issues with providing instructions for this process?

VISIT www.contentfuelframework.com/focuses and click "Process" for a list of helpful tools and additional resources about process focused content

6

Curation

WHEN CURATION is the focus of a content piece, the piece is made up of an intentionally selected list of items, chosen for a specific characteristic or based on specific criteria.

A curated content piece may aim to collect and present a selection of merchandise for sale, items for consideration, information with a common theme, or other related sets. You could curate a list of gift ideas, football players, vacation destinations, historical figures, alien encounters, mobile apps, inspirational quotes, songs, or almost anything else.

The key with curation is to narrow down all possible options and select only those items that meet specific criteria or have chosen characteristics.* While there are some curated

---

* Without selection criteria to narrow down your inclusions, you'd end up with an exhaustive list of items. Such lists may have value as reference material, but they are not curated.

content pieces that do not share or disclose the criteria used to select items featured, most make mention of the logic that was used to narrow down the list to the chosen few.

Some content is curated based on objective curation criteria: the items might be selected based on their size, cost, ratings, distance, or some other data point.

For example, if you were to curate a list of "Movies Starring Meryl Streep," the criteria would be simply that Meryl appeared in the film. But you could also curate the "10 Highest-Grossing Films Starring Meryl Streep," based on which of Meryl's film earned the most at the box office, or the "10 Highest-Rated Films Starring Meryl Streep," based on movie-goer rankings from a particular website.

Other content is curated more subjectively—"my favorites" or "things that I think are good gifts" or "what tasted best to me." These types of pieces, curated based on personal preference, qualify as opinion-focused content; opinion is Focus 10, which we'll explore on page 79.

Curation is a great focus to choose when resources are lacking—whether that be time, money, or something else—because it allows for the selection of a set of existing items to serve as the structure of the piece, rather than having to create an entire content piece from scratch.

Because curated content tends to be a collection of multiple items, the headlines and titles of these types of content pieces often contain a number, a plural noun, or otherwise allude to their curated nature, as below:

- **37 Gifts** Every Recent Grad Would Love
- Did You Miss Any of Our 15 Most Viral **Posts** of the Year?
- Tech's **Top** Founders Share **Tips** For New Entrepreneurs
- Try **These** Hacks to Be More Productive in the Morning

While curation can certainly be done with standalone content pieces, it's also something that many platforms offer as a built-in feature, allowing you to curate content elsewhere. For example, you might create curated playlists of related videos on YouTube,* or curate a collection of songs for a playlist on a music-streaming platform like Spotify.

Examples of Curation-Focused Content

Lots of curated content takes the form of a roundup, selecting and gathering a set of items and then presenting those items in no particular order. While these curated pieces generally have clear selection criteria that unifies the items on the list by some common characteristic, the order in which they are presented is either random or unimportant to the impact of the list.

- A restaurant supply store might create a blog post sharing "10 Genius Tools That Will Save You Time in the Kitchen," including an avocado slicer, a garlic press, and an egg yolk separator, chosen based on the most effective tools for reducing the time needed to complete a common kitchen task.

- A social media conference might create a list of "50 Books Every Social Media Marketer Should Read" before their annual conference, creating a list of relevant books that were written by the event speakers, workshop leaders, and other industry leaders.

A close cousin of the roundup is the ranking, which also creates a list of items, but presents them in an intentional order,

---

* Head to www.youtube.com/melaniedeziel for curated playlists of YouTube videos that will help you tell better stories!

based on specific criteria. For example, the items might be objectively ranked by their price, size, performance, popularity, or score.

- A luxury travel agency might create a ranked list of the 10 most luxurious hotel rooms in the entire world, ranking them in ascending order based on their per-night price, with the most expensive room at the end of the list.

- An educational institution might create a ranked list of the most popular college majors, ranking every single major they offer in descending order—from most popular to least popular—based on how many enrolled students have declared that particular major.

Another common way to curate content is to create a link list that simply links to other sources the audience may be interested in. This might include links to other content you have created, or to outside resources created by others.

- An agency that offers search engine optimization services might create a list of the most helpful SEO books, blogs, courses, events, and podcasts to help their audience find relevant educational resources and connect over their common interests.

- Any blogger would be wise to curate a year-end list of their top or favorite content pieces of the previous 12 months, allowing them to resurface their top content for added attention, draw new attention to pieces that still may have more potential, and highlight all the hard work they and their team did throughout the year.

. . . .

Questions to Consider
When Creating Curation-Focused Content

▶ What items are being curated in this piece of content?

▶ How many items should be included in this content piece?

Would including more or fewer items better serve the topic or the audience?

▶ Is this piece curating owned items, items from others, or a combination?

▶ What criteria will be used to select items for inclusion?

Will the selection criteria be disclosed or explained to the audience?

How or where will the selection criteria be disclosed or explained to the audience?

▶ Will the curated items be presented in a particular order?

Will the order be based on objective criteria or subjective criteria?

Which order makes the most sense for the audience or the subject?

. . . .

VISIT www.contentfuelframework.com/focuses and click "Curation" for a list of helpful tools and additional resources about curation-focused content.

7

Data

CONTENT FOCUSED on data aims to tell a story through the lens of numbers, statistics, trends, or other collections of facts and figures.

Raw data or research generally provides too much information to be useful to most people. The average audience member doesn't have the time, expertise, or desire to sort through large data sets to try to determine what can be learned. The best data-focused content sorts, condenses, analyzes, and repackages the most relevant parts of a data set to create a more easily understood set of insights.

Many data-focused content pieces are based on original research or proprietary data, that is, data that you discover, own, or otherwise control. This might be data about your customers, products, employees, or sales, or it could be data points collected through a study, focus group, or other form of research you conducted yourself.

One of the advantages of conducting original research or using proprietary data is that it allows you to share information for the first time, without competition. When a content piece is the first to share a finding, others who want to discuss or cite that insight are likely to link back to the original, which can help with content discovery, traffic, reputation building, and search ranking.

When there isn't enough original data to justify a standalone piece, data points can still be used to inform, supplement, or complement other content. Oftentimes, these data-focused asides can take the form of a "by the numbers" sidebar, infographic, or other supplementary content element.

For example, if a university were creating a history-focused piece about the longtime dominance of their women's basketball team,* they might include a paragraph or sidebar within that piece that shares some interesting numbers: total championship wins, total Final Four appearances, number of undefeated seasons, longest win streak, or coaches' win percentage.‡

Of course, conducting original research or using proprietary data is not always feasible, due to limited access, limited resources, or privacy concerns. Ensuring that data is accurate, consistent, reliable, and thoroughly verified may require more time, money, tools, or expertise than can be reasonably given to a single project.

---

* I grew up in Connecticut, where the UCONN women's basketball team reigns. My mom had a bumper sticker that read "UCONN: Where men are men, and women are champions."

‡ My Huskies hold all these NCAA records. Look up "UCONN women's basketball" on wikipedia.org for the data.

But not being able to conduct research does not preclude you from creating data-focused content. In fact, some of the most compelling pieces of data-focused content are created by conducting analysis on data collected and shared by others, or by combining several different data sources to surface entirely new connections and insights.

The headlines and titles of data-focused content pieces often contain hints of their focus, with references to the source of the data or allusions to the data itself. Sometimes, terms like "science," "research," or "study" may be used in place of "data," but the implications are generally the same. You'll often find data-focused content with headlines like these:

- **New Study:** Eating Cheese Daily Increases Your Lifespan*
- You've Been Washing Your Face All Wrong, **According to New Research**
- **New Survey Suggests** Teens Are Spending Less Time Online
- **Here's What The Data Says** About Avoiding Divorce
- **What Science Tells Us** About Low-Carb Diets

Examples of Data-Focused Content

The type of data stories that tend to drive the most engagement for the creator is the sharing of original data. Conducting a proprietary study, analysis, focus group, or other research project ensures that the data shared will be the first of its type, without competition, and will likely create greater engagement, earn more citations, and generate a higher return on the time spent to create it.

---

* This is a hypothetical. Please don't change your cheese habits without data from actual cheese scientists.

- A credit card company might conduct a survey of their customers to see which regions spent the most for holiday shopping, which types of gifts were purchased, and how holiday spending compared to years past.

- A security company might conduct an analysis of all the home break-ins logged by their security systems, offering insights on when, where, and how most home invasions occur, helping potential customers identify their vulnerabilities and risk factors.

While plenty of original data pieces are one-offs, conducted or shared only once, others can be repeated at regular intervals to create a recurring report. Many companies do this with annual or quarterly surveys or analysis, fueling the creation of regular reports.

- A financial advisor might create a quarterly report for clients, sharing insights and analysis into the sectors, companies, and industries that are performing well or stagnating.

- A company that sells social measurement software might create an annual report based on customer surveys, showing the shifting trends in social media behavior, activity, attitudes, use, engagement, or spending.

If conducting proprietary research is not an option, data analysis allows for the examination of others' original data to find new insights, uncover trends, or approach a story from a new perspective.

- A real estate agent might combine publicly available data regarding street cleaning schedules, parking pass requirements, and parking citation rates to create her own recommendations of the neighborhoods that are most friendly to car owners.

- A nutritionist might examine several recent studies about vegetarianism, veganism, and plant-based diets to create an article about the benefits of a meat-free diet.

· ·

Questions to Consider
When Creating Data-Focused Content

▶ **Is there an interesting way to tell this story through data, research, or studies?**

Could this topic be approached through the lens of numerical, financial, or other types of trends, projections, or comparisons?

▶ **How might data be collected on this topic?**

▶ **What existing data sets could be analyzed to discover new trends or story ideas?**

▶ **Are resources available to conduct proprietary research or collect new data on this topic?**

Is additional or outside expertise needed to conduct this research correctly?

▶ **What data is freely and publicly available about this topic?**

Is additional data available for a fee or by securing additional rights?

▶ **What credible and qualified people or organizations can provide data on this topic?**

▶ What best practices for data collection, validation, or analysis should be followed?

▶ What level of detail should be provided about how the data was collected?

. . . .

VISIT www.contentfuelframework.com/focuses and click "Data" for a list of helpful tools and additional resources about data-focused content.

8

Product

CONTENT THAT focuses on a product most often serves a sales or marketing goal, where it provides information that guides a potential customer along the journey to becoming an actual customer.

Product-focused content tends to be easiest to understand in the context of a physical product for sale. The best example of this might be the product information page on a company website or on a sales site like Amazon, where you'd find elaborate written descriptions of the product's features, benefits, uses, costs, and more.

You may also find photos of the product, videos of it being unpacked or used, diagrams of the product, reviews, and other helpful information.

And while sales pages for physical products are likely easiest for you to picture, this content focus is not limited to those creators and storytellers with a physical product for sale. You might create product focused content that offers details about services, memberships, access, or other less tangible offerings.

This could include a sales page for your available consulting packages, video testimonials about your dog-walking services, an article previewing an event you'd like people to attend, a preview video of an upcoming webinar you're offering, or even a simple social post wherein you announce and describe an upcoming live-stream conversation you'll be having. All of these focus on something you are offering your audience, and are created with the goal of encouraging conversion.

When content about a product is found on sales or other static web pages, it rarely comes with a headline; instead the presence of product photos, pricing, and other product details indicate the focus. But when the content is more narrative in nature, and does have a headline or title, the headlines generally include a reference to the product itself, or to the experience with it, like so:

- **About** Book/Movie/Author/Product
- **Unboxing** the All-New **Product**
- **Review**: The **New Product** Delivers on Its Promise
- We Tried **Product**: Here's What You Need to Know

In some cases, your "product" may very well be you—yourself—if you are building a personal brand and fan base as an influencer, blogger, speaker, author, or thought leader. In these cases, you may create content that focuses on you, with the goal of building a relationship with your audience. You might create more personal content about yourself, making the relevant calls to action to convert your audience into loyal commenters, subscribers, fans, and followers.

Examples of Product-Focused Content

The most obvious examples of product-focused content are landing pages and sales pages, where the entire focus is on sharing details about products, with the goal of creating a sale or other relevant conversion.

- A thought leader with an online course for sale might create a landing page that provides all the details about the course, including the curriculum, bonuses, price, enrollment period, and testimonials.*

- A software company might create a series of landing pages on their website with details about the packages available, comparing the different features, number of permitted users, support, and other variables within the three price tiers they offer.

But product-focused content also comes in the form of product announcements. While product pages are generally attempting to be fairly exhaustive with product information, announcements are primarily focused on sharing selected new information about a product, such as updates, changes, adjustments, or new releases.

- A company selling consumer packaged goods might create a press release announcing the return of retro packaging and three discontinued flavors for a limited time, with the goal of driving up sales during the month of the promotion.

---

* For example, my Brand Storyteller Mastermind landing page explains what gets covered in the 12-week program, what members get, and when registration opens. See www.brandstorytellermastermind.com.

- An author might create a live video on Instagram or Facebook to share his excitement as he opens the box containing the very first printed copies of his upcoming book, with the goal of building anticipation for its release.

Many brands and companies create product support content, which provides information about product-adjacent details. Often, this comes in the form of FAQ pages, supporting documentation, and other information that may not be needed for all customers, but will be of use to some.

- An appliance company might provide several pieces of instructional content for each appliance they sell, with information about how to clean it, replace parts, and troubleshoot common issues, with the goal of showing how easy the product is to care for.

- A luggage retailer might create a list of travel essentials that match or otherwise fit into their new suitcase, helping customers to see the suitcase they sell as part of their travel experience.

· ·

Questions to Consider
When Creating Product-Focused Content

▸ Will this piece of content be about an in-house product, or a different organization's product?

▸ What information does the audience need to know about this product?

▶ **What questions might the audience have with regards to the product?**

What product questions can be discovered through keyword research?

What product questions are being asked on social media?

What product questions are being asked of sales, customer service, etc.?

▶ **What can be said to dispel any doubts or correct any misconceptions the audience may have about this product?**

▶ **What action or conversion is this piece encouraging the audience to make?**

▶ **Are there ancillary or related products that should be mentioned or acknowledged?**

Are there competitive products that should be mentioned or acknowledged?

. . . .

VISIT www.contentfuelframework.com/focuses and click "Product" for a list of helpful tools and additional resources about product-focused content.

9

Example

WHEN CONTENT is created through the lens of an example, it presents the story or details of a single or specific thing as a means of introducing, demonstrating, or showcasing a broader trend, issue, or story.

Sharing an individual story brings the broader trend or issue into sharper focus for the audience, who may not otherwise be able to fully understand its impact.

In some instances, the example you choose to share can be that of a person whose experience exemplifies the experience many people are having. Hearing the specifics of one individual's life, struggle, or situation allows the audience to better understand the total impact of the broader trend, which might otherwise be difficult to grasp.

Other times, a company or product may be used as an example to illustrate a broader industry trend affecting other similar products and companies. The detailed exploration of a single product, startup, or organization may help bring into focus a trend that applies to many products, startups, or organizations of that type, providing tangible evidence of the impact.

The key difference between using a person or organization to create example-focused content and using that person's story to create people-focused content (as introduced in Focus 1, starting on page 27) is the purpose of the content piece: people-focused content is created with the sole goal of sharing the story of an individual or group, while example-focused content uses those stories primarily as a means to introduce a broader theme, issue, or topic.

Example-focused content pieces typically have a "two-act" structure, where the first part of the piece shares the story of the specific instance, person, or product, and the second part talks about the larger trend that the first story serves to illustrate.

The transitions between the two parts of these example-focused stories often have a similar structure, drawing the connection between the example and the broader trend.

- Person: *"...And while Jane's survival story may be harrowing, it's unfortunately not unique. She is just one of more than 37,000 women who have taken this journey in the last five years..."*

- Company/Product: *"...But the cafe's hockey-stick growth has slowed in recent months. Work & Sip was the first membership-based cafe and coworking space in the city when it opened in 2014, but it's no longer the only game in town for thirsty entrepreneurs and remote workers. There are now 12 such spaces in Smithville alone, with two others set to open..."*

The headlines of example-focused content pieces can vary widely, but they sometimes have a structure that shows how there is a broader phenomenon at the example's core, like these do:

- **What One** Director's Experience **Can Teach Us About** the Film Industry's Gender Imbalance
- **How This** Tiny NYC Shop **Started** the Black Ice Cream **Trend Sweeping the Nation**
- How **Local** Beekeepers **Are Disproportionately Affected** by Global Warming

Examples of Example-Focused Content*

Many example-focused content pieces use the story of an individual person to introduce the situation, struggle, or experience of a larger group of people.

- A local non-profit encouraging eco-friendly activism might share the story of a student who started a recycling program at the town high school, as a way of having a larger conversation about the benefits, growth, and impact of grassroots green initiatives.

- A stylist might create a piece of content sharing how a certain celebrity has successfully embraced green in her wardrobe, as a way of introducing "forest green" as the hottest color of the fall and offering advice on how to adopt the trend.

---

* Well, this section headline got weird, didn't it?

When trying to tell a story about a trend that impacts multiple companies or products, some content starts with the story of a specific company or product to effectively introduce the larger topic.

- A food blogger might write an article sharing the meteoric rise of a new sushi restaurant chain, before transitioning into a broader discussion of the growing Japanese influence on modern American cuisine.

- A venture capital firm might create a blog post telling the story of a successful scooter-sharing startup they helped fund, as a way to open up a larger discussion about the continued growth of the sharing economy.

Another savvy use of example-focused content, particularly for those in marketing, is the narrative testimonial, which offers a detailed account of a single customer or client's experience as a way of introducing the broader impact of a particular product or service.

- A fitness trainer might create a detailed blog post sharing the story of a specific client who lost 108 pounds with her training program, creating a natural opportunity to share some of the other benefits, results, and outcomes she has created for her client base.

- A search engine optimization agency might share the detailed story of one customer who was able to increase revenue dramatically in six months by using their service, as a segue into some broader stats about the results they have created for their customers.

. . . .

Questions to Consider
When Creating Example-Focused Content

- Does this story reflect a common or increasingly frequent experience, situation, or trend?

- Are there individual examples that accurately represent the bigger story?

  Are there people with stories representative of the collective experience?

  Are there companies or products that illustrate the larger trend?

  Are there individual anecdotes that add context to an intangible concept?

- Would focusing on a smaller part of this story, for at least part of the content, make the larger trend easier to understand, contextualize, or relate to?

- Which individual story, person, or other example best represents the larger trend?

- How much detail is necessary for this example to sufficiently explain the larger issue?

- Will the individual example be used to introduce the larger trend, or to add detail and context once the larger trend has been explored?

. . . .

VISIT www.contentfuelframework.com/focuses and click "Example" for a list of helpful tools and additional resources about example-focused content.

10

Opinion

OPINION-FOCUSED content is content created through the lens of a view, belief, or judgement, rather than through the lens of objective facts only.

There can be a lot of value in sharing the perspective, beliefs, and assessments of an individual through opinion-focused content. The audience may be eager to hear your opinion on particular issues, and may value knowing how you feel about a product, trend, or issue. It can help them sort through options, process information, make decisions, or see a point of view they may not have considered otherwise.

Some see opinion content as risky or potentially alienating, because it requires sharing personal views or judgements, which a subset of the audience might disagree with. And while it may be beneficial to plant a flag on one side of a particular issue to reinforce your brand value, most opinion content is much less controversial.

A common form of opinion content is a review, wherein an individual shares their assessment of a product or experience. Many times these reviews will end with a rating ("4.5 out of 5 stars") or a recommendation for the audience, such as "this is a must-buy if you want efficiency below the $100 price point."

If you're not ready, willing, or able to share your views and make such clear recommendations, there are some more subtle approaches to opinion content. One of the easiest ways to experiment with sharing views and judgements is to try to create rankings—that is, placing multiple items in an order.

We first discussed rankings in the chapter on Focus 6: Curation (page 55), but rankings can also be a type of opinion content. The key differentiator is the criteria by which the items are selected or arranged. In the case of opinion rankings, the order is subjective or personal, rather than objective or universal.

For example, if you wrote a blog post titled "The 10 Best Rock Albums of All Time," in which you list and describe the albums that most contributed to your love of rock music, that blog post would be your opinion. Someone else writing this same list would have different albums appearing in a different order, based on their own opinion.

By contrast, if you ordered the list of albums by total sales and called it the "10 Best-Selling Rock Albums of All Time," this would not be opinion-focused content, because it would be a curated list, ranked based on objective data. Different writers of this list should all come up with the very same list of 10, in the same order, because the selection and order are based on a consistent and objective data set—total sales for each album.*

---

* Lists made from out-of-date information or different sources of data might differ, but the point remains that curated content based on objective data is not influenced by personal opinion.

Headlines of opinion-focused content often include first-person language, or otherwise allude to the subjective nature of the content. Potential headlines for opinion-focused content might be:

- What **I** Learned from a Month of Plastic-Free Living
- **My Favorite** Gluten-Free Cookie Recipes
- The 9 **Best** Independent Comedies of the Year
- **Why I'm** Switching Cosmetic Subscription Boxes

Examples of Opinion-Focused Content

Perhaps the most obvious type of opinion content is the review, where an individual or organization expresses their judgements and assessment of a particular product or experience.

- A well-known video blogger might create a video wherein she reviews a new tripod and makes recommendations for her audience about whether to buy it, how to use it, and who it might be right for.

- A mommy blogger might create a written review of a new local theme park after visiting with her young family, sharing what they experienced, how they felt, whether they will return, and whether she thinks her audience should make the trip.

Rankings are similar to reviews in that they create a list of items, assembled and ordered through the lens of subjective criteria, preferences, or judgement.

- A sales trainer and author of sales books might write a blog post sharing his favorite business podcasts, ranked based on which he personally feels are most unique, valuable, and helpful for sales professionals.

- A fashion model might create a video in which she ranks her 10 personal favorite makeup and beauty products, based on which ones help her look awake and feel refreshed even when she's tired or jet lagged.

Other opinion pieces include reflections or personal essays, which are autobiographical in nature and share someone's thoughts on a particular experience they have had. These differ slightly from reviews in terms of goal; the creator likely does not intend the audience to replicate their experience, only to take their lessons from it.

- A genetic testing company might feature a personal essay on their blog titled "What I Learned on My Trip to Discover My Heritage," written by an individual who traveled the world after learning their true ancestry through the company's testing.

- An athlete might share a video documenting her return to the gym and her sport after an injury, sharing her personal journey of pain and growth, what she is learning about her body, and how this experience has changed her.

. . . .

Questions to Consider
When Creating Opinion-Focused Content

▶ Would this content be better if created through the lens of opinion or of fact?

▶ Is the opinion on this topic relevant to the business, brand, or content goals?

▶ Will this content be presented as the opinion of an individual or of an organization?

Is that choice or distinction clear to the audience?

How can this distinction be disclosed or explained to the audience?

▶ What risks may be involved in sharing this opinion with the audience?

Will sharing this opinion split or alienate the audience in an undesirable way?

Does sharing this opinion introduce any legal liability?

Does sharing this opinion show undesirable bias or favoritism?

▶ Is the opinion being shared on this topic informed and fair?

▶ Are there different opinions on this topic that should also be addressed or shared?

. . . .

VISIT www.contentfuelframework.com/focuses and click "Opinion" for a list of helpful tools and additional resources about opinion-focused content.

Content Focus
Cheat Sheet

1   People

2   Basics

3   Details

4   History

5   Process

6   Curation

7   Data

8   Product

9   Example

10 Opinion

VISIT www.contentfuelframework.com/focuses for examples, tools, and additional resources.

THE
10
FORMATS

1

Writing

Now that I've defined the 10 most common content focuses, it's time to switch to examining the formats in which these stories can be brought to life. We're going to start with written content—sequences of letters assembled with the intention of creating coherent words and sentences.

Written content is so ubiquitous that there's a good chance it's the content format you think of by default. There's writing on road signs and billboards, on product packaging and restaurant menus, and in our mailboxes, both digital and physical. Writing fills our social feeds, messaging apps, and the screens of all our devices.

Most people have also had some degree of training in writing, since formal education tends to emphasize it as a means of sharing knowledge and telling stories. Educators teach letters, spelling, grammar, and punctuation as students move through school, being graded as they learn to communicate increasingly complex ideas through writing.

Young children start with three-lined paper, responding to prompts like "What I want to be when I grow up."* High school students type up five-paragraph essays about color symbolism in *The Scarlet Letter*, and divulge their challenges and triumphs in college application essays. Post-secondary students are given 60 minutes to fill Blue Books with midterm essays, and some spend months working on a thesis or dissertation.

Whether we particularly enjoyed these writing exercises or not, it's no surprise that most of us have some degree of fluency in creating written content.

The combination of these two things—the ubiquity of the written word and the training that most of us receive in school—means that writing is also one of the most approachable content formats: you only really need a phone, computer, or pen and paper to get started. Since many of us in content creation roles already have access to one or all of these things, creating written content is often the easiest, fastest, and cheapest format for telling stories.

A key consideration for written content is that it's often most powerful when combined with some of the other formats discussed in the chapters to come. While writing can be an efficient way to communicate stories with an audience, it's not the most eye-catching and it's not often favored by social algorithms when presented alone. To that end, consider written content to be a great starting point, and always ask what

---

* In first grade, I said I would be a WNBA champion, president, and Pope, but I'm a five-foot-three Muslim, so the odds aren't in my favor...

other formats might be powerful supplements to the written content you create.

It's also worth noting that most content, no matter what format it's presented in, will also include writing as an "add-on," because writing is often the vehicle through which content is promoted. Writing forms the basis for most social posts that intend to drive audiences to linked content pieces, and is the default way to add context to photos and videos through things like captions, descriptions, titles, and headlines.

Examples of Written Content

Of all the content formats we'll talk about in the coming chapters, written content is probably the most flexible and transportable, capable of shape-shifting and being packaged in an almost endless number of ways.

One of the most common forms that written content takes is articles and blogs, which often appear in newspapers or magazines, and on websites. Articles and blogs can range in length from just a few hundred words to thousands,* and they generally cover a single topic. Whether print or digital, articles and blogs typically have a headline at the top of the page that indicates what the content is about, and may have subheadings throughout to help organize the content further.

- A company selling project management software might write an article for their website offering tips for maintaining focus and productivity in an open office plan.

---

* In 2013, the New York Times published a 28,000-word article series by Andrea Elliot called "Invisible Child," about homelessness in New York City. It was (at the time) the largest investigative piece NYT had ever run.

- A fitness influencer or health coach might create a blog post about staying healthy over the holidays, with a headline like "Five Healthy Habits to Help You Survive the Holidays."

Sometimes, written content is intended to stand alone and be used for a process, such as with a worksheet, checklist, or guide. These can be printed or digital, and are often offered as free or low-priced downloadable PDF files to supplement an audience's learning on a topic.

- A food blogger might offer a branded "Vegan Shopping List" that offers a written list of recommended products for maintaining a diet free of animal products.

- A corporate consultant or speaker might bring along printed copies of a written guide that summarizes the key takeaways of their keynote or workshop, ensuring attendees remember the main points.

Sometimes written content is assembled into larger and more in-depth content pieces like white papers, reports, and ebooks. These authoritative documents tend to be longer than articles or guides, include research or data-backed recommendations, and are often technical in nature and content.

- Many companies in technical or highly regulated industries publish quarterly white papers that summarize important changes, trends, or happenings in their industry.

- Thought leaders of all types—including social influencers, bloggers, speakers, coaches, and consultants—often create digital-only ebooks to showcase their subject matter expertise instead of (or in addition to) traditionally published print books, because ebooks have a shorter production timeline.

Books—like the one you're reading right now—are, of course, written content, too. These include everything from children and young adult books to romance novels, self-help guides, memoirs, business books, and other non-fiction. Many thought leaders work with a traditional or hybrid publisher to create a book that will showcase their expertise, increase their credibility, and create a new revenue stream.

- A branding consultant or speaker might write a book on the principles of building a brand in the digital age, allowing him to identify himself as an author and sell copies of his books to clients.

- The CEO of a startup that was recently acquired might write a book sharing the lessons she learned hiring a team, growing her company, raising investment from venture capitalists, and preparing her company for sale.

Written content, in the form of web copy or sales copy, also forms the backbone of most websites and other sales materials. On a company or personal website, written content generally communicates most of the basic information about a company's purpose, products, services, team, history, and more.

- A farming equipment company might produce a 20-page printed product catalogue with written descriptions of all products and prices, to be sent to potential customers and passed out at trade shows.

- A dog grooming studio might create a different page for each service they offer, describing what processes the service entails, what tools are used, how pups are looked after during procedures, and why these services are important for a dog's wellness.

I couldn't possibly name every use for the written word, or every way you might possibly use written text to share information and stories with your audience. Your particular industry might require you to create other iterations of written content not addressed here, like a syllabus, catalogue, or instruction manuals for products.

. . . .

Questions to Consider When Creating Written Content

▹ **Who will write this piece of content?**

Will the writer of this content be identified?

How and where will the writer of this content be identified?

▹ **How long should this piece of written content be?**

▹ **What tone of voice will this content be written in?**

▹ **Will this content be edited before it is shared publicly?**

Who will edit the content?

What style or rules will be used to edit the content?

Has edit time been built into the production timeline?

▹ **Is it necessary to translate this content into other languages?**

▹ **Will this content need to be formatted or designed once it's written?**

▹ **Can other content formats be included to add depth or context?**

. . . .

VISIT www.contentfuelframework.com/formats and click "Writing" for a list of helpful tools and additional resources about written content.

2

Infographic

NFOGRAPHICS ARE visual or graphic representations of related information and data pieces, offering a visual overview of a topic in a single, visually appealing file or image. The most engaging infographics use a cohesive color palette to present multiple data points about a single topic, arranging them intentionally with minimal text.

The quality of an infographic depends on the presence of data, of course. Most often, this refers to numerical data, such as statistics, percentages, quantities, measurements, rankings, and similar figures.

But infographics aren't limited to purely numerical data. Many infographics deconstruct processes, places, objects, demographics, trends, and more using iconography, illustration, and other graphic elements.

Because a successful infographic is a mix of data and design, and therefore requires a combination of good research and good visual instincts, infographics often work best when they are created in collaboration between two individuals with these separate skills. A journalist might work to research and compile data points on a particular topic, and be paired with a visual designer who can bring that data to life through compelling and cohesive design.

As discussed in the chapter on data-focused content, the data you use does not necessarily need to be your own proprietary data obtained through studies, focus groups, or other means. As long as you're providing proper credit and citations, compiling data from multiple authoritative sources may actually help you create a more comprehensive and credible infographic.

One of the distinct advantages of creating infographics is that they offer a lot of potential for content repurposing. A single infographic with many data points can be spliced and diced to create many smaller infographics for use on social media.

Examples of Infographic Content

Infographics are a great way for companies and organizations to make complex ideas simple, and to quickly convey a lot of information. Many groups use infographics to share information that their audience, customers, or users would be curious about, but might not be able to access, compile, or determine on their own.

- A sports franchise might create an infographic about each player on their team at the end of the season, sharing their top games, personal records, and season-long stats.

- A fitness tracker company might create an infographic using anonymized user data to reveal which cities in a particular area get the most steps, go to bed earliest, bike the most miles, or eat the healthiest meals.

A very common theme for infographics is "by the numbers" infographics, where a topic that is not typically thought of or explored numerically is broken down to smaller numerical parts.

- An event-planning company might create a recap of each year's conference with a "2020 Summit by the Numbers" infographic, sharing the number of attendees, speakers, sponsors, slideshows, boxed lunches served, cupcakes made, t-shirts handed out, and cups of coffee consumed.

- An airport might promote the opening of a new terminal with a "Terminal C by the Numbers" infographic, with the number of new gates, seats, security checkpoints, moving sidewalks, restaurants, water fountains, lounges, bathrooms, and magazines waiting in the new terminal newsstand.

The vast majority of infographics are static, but an increasing number of creators and storytellers are using coding skills or specialized tools to create interactive infographics—that is, graphics with elements that move, animate, change, or can otherwise be manipulated. Interactive infographics might include:

- tabs or labels that can be clicked to swap between categories or groups of data

- numbers, lines, bars, icons, or other visual elements representing data points that change color, size, shape, or position when they are hovered over or clicked

- a pie chart that allows you to hover over or click on any slice to receive a pop-up with more information

- a sliding scale that allows you to click and drag to adjust the date or time for which data is being displayed

While these types of interactivity are typically limited to infographics that are created and displayed digitally, it's not totally impossible to create similar experiences in print infographics. Oftentimes, these print infographics use some of the same features that offer interactivity in children's books, such as pull-tabs, liftable flaps, and multiple layers.

For example, in 2014, my team at the *New York Times* (a storytelling-focused division of the advertising department, called T Brand Studio) collaborated with Shell Oil to create a digital interactive infographic about the growth of cities around the world. We were able to approximate the experience in print by using two pages—a map printed on regular newsprint, and a second page featuring additional map points printed on semi-transparent vellum. By layering the second page over the top of the first, readers could switch back and forth between the present and future states of the map, creating an "interactive" experience with a print infographic.

. . . .

Questions to Consider When Creating Infographics

▷ What data can be visualized with an infographic?

▷ Is there enough data to justify creating an entire infographic?

Can supplementary data points add greater context?

▷ Can the data be easily visualized using charts, graphs, icons, or other means?

▷ Will this infographic contain any branding?

Does the coloring, language, and iconography complement both the topic and our branding (if needed)?

▷ Can this infographic be cut/adapted for use elsewhere, such as on social media?

▷ How can the sources of the data be made clear in the graphic?

▷ Is the audience likely to view this type of content on a mobile device?

Can this infographic be seen and understood at such a small size?

Can interactivity be triggered effectively at such a small size?

Is an alternate layout or design necessary for mobile devices?

. . . .

VISIT www.contentfuelframework.com/formats and click "Infographic" for a list of helpful tools and additional resources about infographics.

3

Audio

WE'VE ADDRESSED content in formats you can read and see with written content and infographics, and now we're going to examine content you can hear. This is audio content, or content shared in the form of recorded and transmitted sounds.

One of the advantages of audio content is that it can be consumed while the audience is using their eyes and hands for other activities. This makes it a content format that pairs well with written content or visuals to create a multisensory content experience.

When content is audio-only, this means that you—as a creator and storyteller—can tap into time when your audience would otherwise not be consuming content: while they're working out at the gym, walking the dog, getting ready for work, washing dishes, or on their daily commute.

Now, telling stories with audio naturally requires having something worth listening to, whether that's an individual speaking, a conversation between multiple people, or some other process or experience with unique auditory features. Audio should only be used as a format to tell stories when doing so allows us to share something that just can't be transmitted in the same way through written words alone.

Examples of Audio Content

The form of audio content that likely comes to mind first is a podcast. Podcasts are downloadable or streamable installments of audio content, generally released on a set schedule and focused somewhat tightly around a single topic. Episodes in a series generally have a similar structure, length, and tone to help listeners know what to expect and keep them coming back, episode after episode.

The number of Americans who listen to podcasts monthly has grown steadily over the past few years, reaching 26 percent of the population in 2018.* The growth makes sense: while reading or even watching a video requires focused attention, podcasts allow you to consume a good story, learn something new, or go deep into a subject while you are accomplishing other things: cleaning, driving, walking.

Some podcasts have a single regular host who shares their individual thoughts on a topic, while others might have a pair of hosts who banter back and forth. Many podcasts are interview-style, where a host comes back week after week to interview a different guest on *their* particular expertise,

---

* Find this stat at www.edisonresearch.com/infinite-dial-2018.

background, experience, or story. Other podcasts—often those produced by news organizations—use a more complex structure, weaving together segments of music, narration, interviews, and clips from movies, TV, and more.

- A business consultant might host a recurring podcast where she interviews a different entrepreneur each week, getting them to share their journey to becoming a business owner, and offering tips for aspiring entrepreneurs.

- A newspaper might have a nightly podcast where they run through the day's most important headlines, offering a quick summary of the top news items, for their listeners to play "catch up" on their evening commute.

Audio can also be used to create standalone audio experiences. These are most often audio-reproductions of existing works, in the way that most authors of traditionally pub lished books or ebooks also create an audio book so that their audiences can listen to their creation over the course of several hours, instead of reading it. But standalone audio can also include audio-only works, such as lectures, workshops, guided tours, or other spoken sessions.

- A yoga influencer or wellness coach might create a series of free five-minute guided meditation audio recordings to help potential clients and fans practice mindfulness, and produce a series of hour-long guided meditations for more advanced students of mindfulness to purchase.

- Many museums, universities, and historical landmarks make guided audio tours available on physical headsets or via apps, allowing patrons to explore and learn at their own pace, on their own time, and in their own language, without having to wait for a live tour guide.

Another use case for audio content is offering audio alternatives to content, or including an audio option for consuming content presented in another format. This is an easy way to offer your audience multiple options for consuming a piece of content, based on their available time or technology, or their preferred learning style.

- A coach who uploads videos of their weekly coaching calls might also export the audio of that call, and have it transcribed, allowing his students to choose to engage with the video call by watching or listening, *or* by reading it.

- A blogger might embed an audio player on a blog post, allowing page visitors to read the blog post *or* listen to it being read.

Environmental audio often appears in conjunction with a written piece, and is used to set a scene or share a sound in a way that would be difficult to achieve in writing alone. Environmental audio allows the audience to hear the hard-to-describe features of a subject's quote, such as their tone of voice, accent, or the power of their pauses while speaking. Environmental audio can also be helpful when discussing very similar or unfamiliar sounds, and also for setting a mood or transporting the audience to another place.

- A travel blogger writing an online diary of her trip to the Amazon might include some sound bites so her fans can hear the unique noises of the rainforest themselves, rather than having to rely only on written descriptions.

- A mechanic could create playable clips of common sounds that come from cars, to help drivers identify whether they have a serious problem that needs a professional's assistance or if the issue is something they can fix themselves with a trip to the auto-parts store.

These are the ways that most individuals and brand creators bring audio content to life in the modern era, but you could also include more traditional uses for audio, such as the production of songs and full-on radio shows. My guess is that few will see these as viable options, but if you've got a great singing voice or access to a radio broadcast studio, feel free to experiment with ways to bring your content and stories to life in these ways, too.

. . . .

Questions to Consider When Creating Audio

▶ **Does the story have unique sound elements that require the use of audio?**
What sounds might be difficult to describe or understand without audio?
Could environmental sounds be used to set the scene?

▶ **Is the location or environment conducive to capturing quality audio?**

▶ **Is this a one-off piece of audio content or a recurring series (like a podcast)?**

▶ **Is special talent, software, or equipment needed to capture audio content?**

➤ Is special talent, software, or equipment needed to edit audio content?

➤ Is special talent, software, or equipment needed to host or distribute audio content?

➤ Does the audience have the technology needed to consume audio content?

➤ Can audio be extracted from video to offer an alternative way to consume the story?

· ·

VISIT www.contentfuelframework.com/formats and click "Audio" for a list of helpful tools and additional resources about audio content.

4

Video

VIDEO REFERS to moving images captured and recorded for the purpose of projecting, sharing, distributing, or otherwise viewing content.

For the first part of its history, video was an elite, exclusive, and inaccessible content format, reserved for motion pictures, broadcast news, and other high-production programming that would be televised or shown in theaters. Video cameras, video editing technology, and video distribution processes were all prohibitively expensive and required specialized training to operate.

But most of those barriers have disappeared in recent years. Creating video content has become significantly more approachable and affordable, now that many of us have the ability to easily capture decent quality video on our computers or phones. The internet allows us to freely host and distribute video content without the need for a broadcast station license or a film studio's support, and also ensures that most of us can access and learn video editing software, if needed.*

Digital videos are typically hosted in just one place—the specific site or platform where they are first uploaded and found. But often videos are also shared out to many other online destinations using links or embed codes that allow people to discover and watch the video on other sites and platforms.

For example, you might choose to upload and host your video on YouTube. You might then share that link on Facebook, Twitter, on your blog, or in an email, inviting people to watch the video on YouTube. You might also embed or upload the video on any of these platforms directly, so that the audience can watch and share it without having to click over to YouTube at all.

Attempting to share the specifics of every place and platform where video can live would be an effort in futility in an unchanging format like this book; social networks, platforms, and technologies are always changing, as is the list of which ones are popular, functioning, and preferred.

Instead, this chapter will offer some more common structures and approaches for video content that can be used across platforms and executed according to many different sets of specifications.

Regardless of its length or where it lives, video content is on the rise, with more people creating video each and every year—in fact, more video is now uploaded every month than

---

* Access is relative. But overall we have more access to video cameras, free/open-source video editing software, and tutorials for learning how to use both.

has been created by US television networks during the past 30 years.* Video also captures a huge amount of attention; people spend much more time on content pages containing video than they spend on content pages without video.‡

Many of the social platforms used to distribute content now have a preference for serving up video content, given how much more engaging it tends to be.

Examples of Video Content

A common style of video is a vlog or talking head video, where an individual sits in frame—generally visible only above the waist—and directly addresses the camera and the viewers. While these types of videos may have other segments or sections that don't feature the speaker, they are primarily a one-way conversation where the speaker is sharing their experience, thoughts, opinions, or advice with viewers.

- A fashion model with a growing presence on YouTube might create weekly videos where he appears in front of the camera to share his outfit choices for the week, share some health and fitness advice, and talk about what's happening in his personal life.

- A bank might produce a video where one of their financial advisors sits behind a desk and directly addresses viewers to offer a thorough explanation of how a credit score is calculated and what you can do to increase or protect it.

---

* Find this stat at www.insivia.com/50-must-know-stats-about-video-marketing-2016.

‡ You can learn more about how video impacts time spent here: www.wistia.com/learn/marketing/video-time-on-page.

A common style of video is a narrated or voiceover video, where a speaker directly addresses the viewers from off camera, while showing coordinating video footage of something other than themselves on the screen. This structure works well when the narrator is offering commentary on some other video footage, and it's also helpful for instructional content where supplementary visuals may be necessary to fully explain a process.

- A television reviewer might create a video recapping the last season of a show just before the new season premieres, offering his take on the top plot points while showing clips and still images from those episodes.

- A tech expert might create a video in which she unboxes a new product she just received, or takes a product apart to create a fix for a common problem. While the product and her hands are showing on screen, her voiceover provides further context with her thoughts or instructions.

Sometimes these voiceover videos do not even include video footage, but might instead show a series of photographs, slides, charts, animations, illustrations, or other non-video visuals while an audio voiceover plays.

- A manufacturing company might have an animated explainer that deconstructs one of their machines, taking you inside it while an engineer from one of their manufacturing facilities narrates the explanation of each machine part and each step in the production process.

- A financial advisor might create a video that shows a series of static charts, graphs, and mathematical equations, while her voiceover provides context for how these numbers impact your finances.

Another common video type is an interview video, which captures a recorded conversation between two or more people. Some interviews simply feature multiple individuals sitting together on-screen, asking and answering questions in turns, but often the interviewer is not shown or heard—the subject is simply asked questions from off-screen.

- A company might share a video from their founder's recent appearance on a local TV news program to discuss their product, share their story, and announce an upcoming new feature.

- A podcast team might capture their guest interviews on video, either in-person in a studio or via video-conferencing software, allowing them to offer both visuals and audio of their conversation with their guest.

You might also experiment with "docu-style" videos, which take inspiration from documentary films but are typically shorter in length. These generally focus on a real-life place, person, event, or issue, and provide broad context for that theme through a mix of footage types and styles that might include interviews, on-scene footage, archival footage, graphics and data visualization, narration, and more.

- A chain of restaurants might produce a ten-minute docu-style video introducing their new head chef, including:
  - footage of the chef explaining her food philosophy in the restaurant kitchen
  - interviews with various restaurant executives sharing why they chose the new chef
  - footage of the chef picking ingredients on a farm, while she discusses recipes in a voiceover
  - home video of the chef pretending to cook as a child
  - interviews with family members sharing the chef's long-time passion for food

These video styles and structures don't represent every possible way you could leverage moving images to communicate with your audience, but they should help provide some inspiration for the various common structures that might bring your ideas to life.

Other video structures and constructions you might consider include time-lapse videos—which capture a slow process over time, then digitally speed it up so that it appears to unfold at a much faster pace—and music videos, where songs are artistically paired with video footage and imagery that might relate to the lyrics or theme of the song.

. . . .

Questions to Consider When Creating Video

▸ Is special talent, software, or equipment needed to capture video content?

▸ Is special talent, software, or equipment needed to edit video content?

▸ How long does the video need to be to effectively tell this story?
Would several smaller videos better serve the audience?

▸ Should the video be shot horizontally or vertically, to best fit its intended destination?

▸ Have captions been added to ensure accessibility?

➤ **Is the lighting sufficient to capture quality video in this environment?**

Would supplemental artificial lighting be helpful?

➤ **Would on-screen text, charts, or other graphics add to this video?**

➤ **Would background music or sound effects add to this video?**

Are additional rights needed to use such audio?

➤ **Which platform should this video be posted or hosted on?**

➤ **Which keywords should be used in the video title, description, and tags to optimize this video's discoverability through search?**

• • • ♦ • • • • • • • • ♦ •

VISIT www.contentfuelframework.com/formats and click "Video" for a list of helpful tools and additional resources about video content.

5

Live Video

LIVE VIDEO, also called streaming video, refers to digital video content that is being captured and viewed in real time.

In many ways, live video is extremely similar to the pre-recorded video content we discussed in the previous chapter. Live video combines moving visuals and audio, and can be presented in the form of a vlog, interview, voiceover, and more.

But there are some key differences between pre-recorded and live-streamed video. While pre-recorded video benefits from a careful editing process that eliminates anything undesired, live video doesn't have that advantage: it's often less formal, less consistent, and a little more unpredictable.

Individuals appearing on live-streams tend to speak in a more conversational tone and use more natural language than those on pre-recorded video, since live video is rarely fully scripted. And while the lack of "second takes" might result in more "*ums*" making it to the screen or a few more unplanned tangents, the free-flowing conversation also allows for impromptu responses to viewer questions, the ability to change course in response to viewer feedback, and other benefits.

Often, live video is produced using nothing more than a hand-held device, which can occasionally make for a shaky camera, inconsistent lighting, or poor audio quality. The need for a stable internet or cellular connection also means that live-streams are sometimes victims of freezing visuals, lagging or distorted audio, pixilation, or other connection issues.

And it's not just technical issues that can impact live-streaming. A fire truck could drive by, drowning out the audio with its siren, or a nearby barking dog might be a total distraction for host and viewers alike. The host might drop their phone, forget what they were saying, or mistakenly hit a button that makes undesired changes to the stream.* A rude viewer or passionate host might get carried away, resulting in cursing, inappropriate language, off-topic discussions, or other comments that you never intended to broadcast.

Many of these risks can be mitigated with proper preparation and training, equipment testing, and a smooth host able to go with the flow. But the unpredictability actually has its perks, too.

Because it tends to be more casual and less produced, live video may be perceived by many viewers as more authentic, which could create stronger feelings of familiarity with those on-screen. For those trying to create deep connections with

---

* Wait, you didn't want a bunny-ear filter on your CFO for that live stream?

an audience or fan base, live video might be an even more powerful tool than pre-recorded video.

Increasingly, streaming software, tools, and platforms are also offering features that help mitigate live video risks, and make the live-streams look more polished. Stabilizing cameras and tripods are helping to make shaky hand-held streams a thing of the past, and many live-streaming tools now offer the ability to dynamically supplement live-streams with on-screen text, polls, visual effects, sound effects, and more.

Examples of Live Video Content

Digital live video is commonly used for observation, where a live-stream serves to transmit an event, exactly as it's happening, to others who can't be physically present.

Observation-style videos are, in many cases, similar to live TV news. Just as TV stations would take cameras on scene so viewers can watch a politician's speech or a police chase unfold live, now everyday individuals can stream the events they witness, too. This includes planned events like concerts, sports, parades, and conference presentations, as well as smaller, impromptu, or day-to-day events they encounter, such as a street performance, a house fire, or a sunrise.

- A zoo might set up a live-stream aimed at the eggs inside the nest of a rare bird, allowing animal lovers to watch the next generation hatch, as it happens.

- An event planner may set up a live-stream from the back of an auditorium, allowing remote audience members to observe a speaker, panel, or other presentation even if they can't be physically in the room

But many of the structures discussed for pre-recorded video in the previous chapter—including vlogs, narrated videos, and interviews—can also work in the form of live video, with relatively little adaptation.

- **Vlog**: An interior design expert might do a weekly live-stream where they sit at their desk and answer viewer-submitted questions about decor, design, home organization, minimalism, avoiding clutter, and more.

- **Narrated Video**: A chef or food blogger might turn on a live stream as they walk through the farmers' market, showing what local ingredients are available at each farm stand and explaining how they know which items are ripe enough to take home.

- **Interview**: A marketing consultant might conduct live-streamed video interviews with other marketing experts, creating a weekly "live podcast" or "digital talk show."

When it's selected and used strategically, live video offers brands and individuals a chance to offer their audience unprecedented access to events, places, and people, including themselves.

· ·

Questions to Consider When Creating Live Video

➣ Does this video benefit from being captured in real time or having live interaction?

If not, would the audience be better served with a standard (non-live) video?

➣ Is the connection to the internet or cellular network strong enough and stable enough to support the uninterrupted streaming of live video?

What can be done to improve the connection?

➣ Are the equipment, lighting, and sound sufficient for necessary content quality?

How can the risk of interruptions, both real and digital, be minimized?

➣ Which platform is best to host this live video?

Which platform best captures the intended audience?

Which live video platform offers needed/desired features?

➣ How will this video be promoted or distributed to encourage live viewing?

Which tools will broadcast this live content to multiple platforms at once?

How could the video be promoted in advance?

How could the live broadcast be distributed to drive up live viewing?

➤ **What opportunities and tools will promote engagement with the live audience?**

What tools provide for engaging with live-stream viewers?

What questions, prompts, or other calls to action will encourage engagement?

What tools or rules will be used to moderate viewer comments or engagement?

➤ **How will this content be repurposed once the live broadcast has ended?**

➤ **Have all the questions from the previous chapter on Format 4: Video also been taken into account?**

. . . .

VISIT www.contentfuelframework.com/formats and click "Live Video" for a list of helpful tools and additional resources about live video content.

FORMAT

Image Gallery

AN **IMAGE** gallery is simply a collection of images, generally united by their connection to a common theme or subject.

Image galleries come in all sizes, from four-photo batches uploaded in a social media post to a 200+ image gallery containing every photo from a specific event.

In most instances, image galleries that are intended for public consumption will also be accompanied by writing that offers greater context for the images and their subjects. This text serves to describe the action occurring in the image, identify the individuals represented, offer credit to the creator of the image, or provide other information related to the image's origins, content, or significance.

Sometimes the accompanying writing comes in the form of brief captions located underneath or alongside each of the images. Other times, larger occlions of text—up to several paragraphs—may separate each of the images, creating a content piece that feels closer to an article.

As the quality of cameras and amount of storage available on most smartphones has increased in recent years, it has become increasingly easy for almost any individual to capture quality images. Image galleries, as a result, are an easy supplemental format that can be added to content that is primarily presented in another format.

Examples of Image Gallery Content

Content presented in an image gallery is frequently presented as an image list, where a set number of images appear on a single page, such that you could see all of the images without having to click away to another page. Image lists tend to come in one of two varieties: ranked and unranked.

In a ranked image list, the images are ordered in a particular way, such that an image's position on the list indicates its relation to the others. Whether the list is ranking the images themselves, or instead ranking the people, places, or things that the images depict, the image order is intended to convey each item's place in a hierarchy.

Often these ranked image lists are focused on superlatives—top, best, worst, most, least—and the ordering of the images indicates the list creator's opinion about how the included images rank in relation to the others.

- A sports blogger and commentator might compile a ranked image list of the "21 Most Amazing Photos from the Olympics," sharing pictures of impressive athletes captured at just the right time during the Games.

- A lipstick company might create a post on their company blog featuring a ranked image list of what they deem to be the "10 Best On-Screen Kisses of All Time," matching each of these iconic movie moments to a lip color they offer.

In an unranked image list, the image order does not necessarily indicate the images' relation to one another (or the relation of the people, places, or items that the images represent). While the images may have been ordered with intention, and the list may even include numbers in its headline or structure, these numbers and ordering do not attempt to convey a sense of hierarchy.

- A network marketer selling health and fitness products might create an unranked image list of "13 Smoothie Recipes You'll Want to Add to Your Morning Routine" to show some of the easy and appetizing recipes that can be created using the products he promotes.

- A chiropractor might create an image list on her blog featuring diagrams of various yoga stretches she recommends for back pain relief, in no particular order.

Another common structure for an image gallery is a slideshow. The content of a slideshow may be exactly the same as an image list, except slideshows display images one at a time in a predetermined order, instead of all at once. With slideshows, viewers navigate through the images individually by swiping through them, clicking a "next" button, or tapping arrow icons.

Like image lists, slideshows also come in ranked and unranked varieties, where the order of the photos is either intended to depict their relation to one another, or not.

- A Hollywood agent might create a blog post featuring a slide-show of her event photos called "Behind the Scenes at the Oscars: 36 Candid Celeb Snapshots," helping showcase how connected she is to the movers and shakers of her industry.

- A hairstylist might create a slideshow for his website featuring before-and-after shots of the clients he has provided remarkable hair transformations for, allowing viewers to click through to reveal each "after" shot.

While lists and slideshows represent the vast majority of image galleries, there are other arrangements for images, to be sure.

In print, for example, many newspapers and yearbooks feature full-page spreads with collages of related images from a specific event, day, or other subject. You might also arrange and display a gallery of images into a printed coffee table book or pamphlet for your business.

And, of course, you could call a collection of framed photos artfully arranged on the wall in your home a gallery, too, united around the theme of your family, pets, favorite flowers, or vacation photos.

. . . .

Questions to Consider When Creating Image Galleries

▸ Are there enough related images to justify creating a gallery?

▸ Is it necessary to secure additional rights to the images needed for this gallery?

▸ Does it matter if the images are the same size, shape, or orientation?

▸ Would the audience prefer to explore these images one by one, or all at once?

▸ Do the images need to be viewed in a specific order?

What order provides the most value for the audience?

Does the order need to be explained or disclosed to the audience?

▸ Can the image gallery be seen and navigated easily on a mobile device?

Is an additional layout or design necessary for a mobile audience?

▸ Where will captions and other supporting information be displayed?

. . . .

VISIT www.contentfuelframework.com/formats and click "Image Galleries" for a list of helpful tools and additional resources about image galleries.

7

Timeline

TIMELINES LEAVE little to the imagination with their naming: they are graphic representations of the passage of time, typically plotted on a line.

Because most of us picture the passage of time as happening from left to right, there's a good chance your default image of a timeline is a horizontal timeline, where the oldest points are plotted the furthest to the left, and the most recent points are plotted furthest to the right.

And while it's true most timelines are presented horizontally, vertical timelines can work in a digital environment, revealing the plotted points one by one as viewers scroll from the top of a page to the bottom.

Most often, timelines are presented in chronological order, such that viewers or readers start at the oldest plotted occurrence on the timeline, then move through history to the most recent plotted point. But some stories may be better served by a reverse-chronological order timeline, which starts in the present day and moves backward through time, point by point, to unpack a trend, retrace our steps, or see what led to the present situation.

Most often, timelines work best in an interactive format, because interactivity allows the audience to explore the timeline at their own pace, skipping points they find less interesting and going back to previously viewed points for clarification as needed.

Examples of Timeline Content

Timelines are a sort of super-format, serving as the backbone or structure by which smaller snippets of content in other formats are arranged or organized.

- A restaurant chain may create an interactive timeline of their history for their website, including events like:

  - the date the co-founders met, with a written description of their meeting
  - the date the head chef was hired, with a photo showing the first menu
  - the date the first location opened, with a video of their first commercial
  - the date they became profitable, with an infographic showing revenue growth
  - the date they opened a second location, with audio of the radio ad announcing its opening

You can also add supplementary timelines into projects that primarily use other content formats. This is particularly helpful when content presented in writing happens in a very particular sequence that might otherwise be hard to follow or remember.

- An appliance company launching a new refrigerator model might create a timeline allowing customers to explore the evolution of refrigeration technology, to show all the history and innovation that went into the latest product.

- A wellness company conducting a video interview with a customer who has experienced dramatic weight loss with their product might play the customer's spoken description of that journey while displaying a timeline that shows a photo of their progress at each point in time.

. . . .

Questions to Consider When Creating Timelines

▶ Does this story take place over a stretch of time, making it well-suited to a timeline?

▶ What time period will this timeline cover?

When will the timeline begin and end?

How will points between the beginning and end be labeled? (Days? Years?)

▶ Will this timeline be presented horizontally or vertically?

▶ Will this timeline's points be presented in chronological or reverse-chronological order?

▶ Will this timeline be static or interactive?
How will the timeline be navigated or experienced by its users?

▶ What other content formats can be integrated into the timeline?

▶ Is special research needed to find information and content assets for the timeline?

▶ Are there libraries, historical societies, or other organizations and resources that would be helpful for compiling and finding this historical information?

. . . .

VISIT www.contentfuelframework.com/formats and click "Timelines" for a list of helpful tools and additional resources about timelines.

Quiz

QUIZZES HAVE long been used as a method of knowledge assessment in education. You probably remember taking quizzes in school, whether they came in the form of photocopied question sheets passed around the room or in timed assessments taken online.

Generally speaking, quizzes are used for collecting a set of responses from participants, and then returning a customized score or results based on the participant's individual responses.

Quizzes are a highly engaging and interactive format, allowing you to test your audience's knowledge, drive traffic to educational content that fills knowledge gaps, provide customized recommendations of products, and grow and reward loyalty by engaging users in your message.

The most common quiz question type is multiple choice, where each question has a pre-written list of potential answers, from which a participant selects one or more as correct, based on the instructions. Multiple-choice questions often have three to five answer choices:

How are you currently consuming this book?*

a   Reading a physical book/paper copy
b   Using an e-reader/device to read a digital copy
c   Using a device to listen to the audio version
d   Other method

A close relative of the multiple-choice question is the A/B question, or the yes/no question. These questions are structured and answered similarly to multiple-choice questions, but include only two possible answer choices:

Are you currently reading a physical book/paper copy of this book?

a   Yes, I am
b   No, I am not

Most digital quizzes—like many standardized tests in academic settings—use multiple-choice or A/B questions because the answers are limited and pre-defined, making them easier to collect and correct in a unified, organized, and automated way.

Some quizzes include matching questions, where a participant is provided with two lists and asked to correctly

---

* No matter which form you consume this book in, thanks for taking the time to do so!

match items from one list with the corresponding items in the second list. These lists can be any length, from just a few items to 20 or more.

Match the book format to its corresponding consumption style.

1 Physical/paper book   a Read
2 Digital book   b Listen
3 Audio book   c Read

Some quizzes also use open-ended or fill-in-the-blank questions, which do not provide any answer options and allow participants to write in their own answer.

How are you currently consuming this book? _____

Because answers are less predictable in this format, these types of questions often require human analysis or correction, making them harder to evaluate at scale.

There are also many ways to deliver the results of a quiz. The easiest and most user-friendly is to simply display the results immediately on the same page on which users complete the quiz. However, it's sometimes necessary or beneficial to collect contact information—such as an email address—from the participant, so that you can deliver the results in a more private or personal fashion.

Examples of Quiz Content

Scored quizzes are those where questions have both correct and incorrect answers. Points are awarded for correct answers only, so users attempt to submit as many correct answers as possible to maximize their score. The outcome of the quiz is a score, calculated based on the number of correct answers.

· An airline or travel blogger might create a quiz called "How Much Do You Really Know About Air Travel?" asking a series of questions about airline terms, plane technology, flight safety, or airport protocols.

· A television studio or streaming platform might create a quiz inviting you to "See How Much of a Superfan You Really Are," asking questions about a specific show's characters, plot lines, or actors.

Scored quizzes can also have non-numeric results, so long as those results still correspond to final scores based on right and wrong answers. In the above example of a quiz testing your knowledge of air travel, numeric results might display "92% correct" and praise your accuracy, while non-numeric results might call anyone with accuracy greater than 90 percent "A Master Pilot," and provide a few sentences of catchy copy about how well they know their stuff.

Another common style of quiz is a personality quiz, where there are no incorrect answers, but instead each answer corresponds to one of several potential outcomes. The reader is asked to select their personal preference on a given theme from a set of options for each question, and their answers are combined to categorize them into one of several results.

This is the style of quiz most popular in magazines:* You answer a set of five to 10 multiple choice questions, and then

---

* No teen TV drama or romantic comedy is complete without a reference to a "Cosmo Quiz" that confirms the main characters' true feelings.

add up how many times you answered A, B, C, and D to deter-mine which of the four lettered outcomes is "you."

· A running shoe company might create a quiz that asks about running habits—run length, run frequency, average speed, running goals, pain points—and recommend a particular shoe type or model that would best match that runner's needs.

· A wine company might create a quiz that asks a series of questions about your tastes—if you like red or white wines, if you prefer sweet or salty snacks—and then recommend a particular wine that you would be likely to enjoy.

It's worth noting here that the personality quizzes that provide the most value to the audience are those where audience-provided answers meaningfully correspond to actual outcomes or results.

That being said, there are certainly tons of quizzes that are more *fun* than *function*—where there's really no science, data, or logical connection between an audience member's set of answers and the outcome or results they are given.

. . . .

Questions to Consider When Creating Quizzes

▷ Is a quiz the best way to get the audience to engage with this information?

▷ Is this quiz in service of the audience, in service of a sale, or both?

Do any results lead to call to action or product recommendation?

Do different quiz answers truthfully create different results?

▶ **What information or data is this quiz and its results based on?**

▶ **Is this quiz assessing knowledge (scored) or categorizing participants (personality)?**

  If this is a scored quiz, will results be numeric or non-numeric?

  If this is a personality quiz, how many possible results categories will there be?

▶ **What question type is best for this quiz?**

  Will multiple question types be used?

▶ **How and when will quiz results be delivered?**

▶ **Will user results, contacts, or other data be retained after they are communicated to users?**

  Are we required to disclose data storage to users or to obtain consent? How will we disclose this data storage or obtain consent?

  What security measures should be taken to protect this data?

  How long will this data be stored or maintained?

. . . .

VISIT www.contentfuelframework.com/formats and click "Quiz" for a list of helpful tools and additional resources about quizzes.

Tool

A **TOOL, TO** put it most simply, is an implement designed to carry out a particular function.

When we hear the word "tool," most of us think of the kinds of tools you find in your garage or under the kitchen sink: hammers, screwdrivers, pliers, those little L-shaped Allen wrenches you use to put together Ikea furniture. These tools are designed to insert, tighten, loosen, grab, or secure.

But there are also many tools—digital tools in particular—that are designed for purposes other than construction, destruction, or repair. These digital tools carry out less physical functions, by helping users calculate, convert, and otherwise retrieve and discover useful information.

Tools can be used to project, predict, combine, compare, assess, analyze, identify, and more. This means that a tool is a particularly good format choice when you're creating content about something that includes data, numbers, or trends.

Most of the tools that content creators design are conceived of in response to a direct audience requirement: creators are aware that the audience has a need, and then design a tool that satisfies that need by performing a function or providing necessary information.

To that end, most digital tools require some level of user action or input in order to carry out their function and provide the promised information. By filling in the blanks with their particular information, the audience is able to secure personalized outputs based on the information they have put in.

Some tools take in and process numerical data, performing mathematical equations on the information. Calculators, for example, are common in the financial industry, in particular: a quick internet search will show you hundreds of free online calculators that allow you to estimate or project interest accrual, credit changes, loan terms, mortgage or tax payments, insurance premiums, investment returns, retirement growth, and other financial values.

A close cousin of the calculator is the converter, which takes in information of one unit type, then provides corresponding information of another unit type. Although converters often process numerical data, some can create equivalencies between non-numerical information, too. Some common examples of this tool type might be a time zone converter, a currency converter, or translation tool that converts text from one language to another.

Other tools take in and process data such as text or images. There are lots of useful text analysis tools for writers and content creators that allow you to enter bodies of text to calculate character count, determine the reading level, check for plagiarism, and more.

There are also a variety of photo tools designed to perform specific functions on uploaded photos of your face: some show what you would look like aged forward, as the opposite gender, or with different hair and makeup styles, while others might try to predict what your offspring will look like or show your celebrity doppelgangers.

It's worth noting that while this chapter is primarily focused on exploring and providing examples of digital tools—because of the ease of creating and distributing them—tools *can* be physical, as well.

For example, if you've ever spent time in an OB/GYN's office, you may have seen the cardboard "pregnancy wheel" tool that doctors use to calculate dates of conception, due dates, and various other pregnancy milestones.* The inner cardboard circle lists the milestones with their average spacing, and the outer dial features a calendar. By lining up a specific milestone on the inner dial with its known date on the outer calendar dial—such as the date of the last menstrual period—a doctor can see which calendar dates on the outer dial correspond with all other future milestones on the inner dial.

Examples of Tool-Based Content

Calculators, which take in numerical data and perform mathematical equations on them, can be useful tools for engaging audiences, making projections, or helping process numerical data, even outside of the financial industry.

---

* When you're 33 weeks pregnant and trying to finish your content book before the little one arrives, you start to see relevant examples everywhere!

- A wedding planner might create a calculator that allows couples to enter their total wedding budget, and provides a percentage-based breakdown of how much they can spend on each element of the big day, from food and decorations to invitations and wardrobe.

- A contractor, interior designer, or home improvement store might provide a calculator that allows renovators to enter the dimensions for a space to receive an estimate of how many cans of paint, boxes of tile, or containers of other supplies they might need to buy in order to complete a specific project.

Converters are another common tool choice. While there may not be much value in creating your own duplicate version of those exact converter tools—which are plentiful and available with a quick web search—there may be converters specific to your story, product, or brand that would be useful for the audience.

- A fashion company might create a size converter that allows you to select your size at several other retailers to find the correct size for their products.

- A hair dye company, nail polish brand, or fabric manufacturer might create a color converter that converts a product number from a competing brand to help shoppers find the coordinating code in their own color-naming system.

Photo processing tools can be used both for fun and for more practical functions. These include the facial recognition apps mentioned earlier that provide entertaining age, gender, or other manipulations, but they can also have incredibly useful utilities.

- An eyewear provider might create a tool that lets clients take or upload a photo of their face and virtually "try on" various glasses frames, to see how they look with their face shape.

- A home improvement store or furniture company may create a tool that invites users to upload a photo of a room to see how different types of flooring, furniture, or light fixtures might fit in the space.

Text processing tools may not be as common as some of the others listed here, but there are still opportunities to create utility for your audience and help get your message across in the form of a tool.

- An organization trying to raise awareness for particular unconscious habits or biases might create an email plug-in designed to scan emails for specific words and phrases, to alert users to potentially problematic language.

- A language learning app, tourism board, or academic institution might create a tool that prompts students or travelers to enter text in another language to test their proficiency.

There are countless other tool types, outside of these categories, that can be used to convey useful or entertaining information. The following examples reflect other types of tools that might enrich your engagement with your audience, or expand your audience's ability to engage with other content types you're already creating.

- An entertainment journalist doing a story about how baby naming trends reflect the popularity of celebrities or television characters might create a tool that lets readers enter their name to see which pop-culture influencers may have led to its popularity

- A chain of gyms, a supplement manufacturer, or an athletic wear company might create a tool that lets customers input current and desired health statistics, so that it can, in turn, provide a customized nutritional plan or workout routine.

· ·

Questions to Consider When Creating Tools

▻ Would the audience benefit from the ability to engage with this story or its data?

▻ What audience questions, problems, or needs could be solved with tools?

Which of these questions can be discovered through keyword research?

Which can be discovered through social media?

Which can be discovered through the audience's interactions with sales, customer service, etc.?

▻ Will the tool process numerical data or non-numerical data?

▻ What information needs to be collected to perform this utility?

▻ How will the necessary information be collected?

▻ How will the results be delivered or communicated?

▷ **Will user results or data be retained after they are communicated to users?**

Are we required to disclose data storage to users or obtain consent? How will we disclose this data storage or obtain consent?

What security measures should be taken to protect this data?

How long will this data be stored or maintained?

· ·

VISIT www.contentfuelframework.com/formats and click "Tool" for a list of helpful tools and additional resources about tools.

FORMAT

10

Map

A **MAP IS** a diagram that visually represents a specific area and all the features of that area that are relevant for the map's intended use. Maps can represent large areas, such as the road system of an entire country, or small areas, such as a walking trail inside a specific local park. Their purposes can vary widely and they can be created using a variety of visual styles and tools.

Most of us are familiar with geographic maps, generally intended as navigational tools. We use these types of maps when we boot up the GPS to get driving directions to a friend's home, open up an interstate atlas on the car hood during a road trip, or drag a finger across a giant mounted sign to trace the path to the correct gate at the airport, stop on the train line, or retail store at the mall.

Storytellers, marketers, or creators may have occasion to create navigational maps that help audiences go on adventures or reach desired destinations. But maps can also be created for purposes other than navigation.

Thematic maps depict specific attributes, characteristics, behaviors, or facts about areas, rather than the geographic particulars of the area itself. Because thematic maps aim to depict primarily non-geographic data, they are often minimal in their geographic labels, providing only as much detail as needed to meaningfully plot their primary data points. Thematic maps are often color coded, allowing viewers to easily spot majorities, see trends, or make comparisons.

For example, a map depicting election results might only include outlines of voter districts—without any streets, city names, or other labels—since the true purpose is to show voter behavior, rather than geographic details of the area where voters took action. By using one color for each candidate, viewers could easily see which regions voted for which candidate, which candidate secured more of the regions' votes, and whether any candidate's votes were clustered in particular regions.

Proximity maps provide geographic context for a story that might be hard to understand without visual guidance. Reference maps are not intended as tools to aid in navigation and, unlike thematic maps, don't usually depict unified data sets across a region. Instead, these maps act more like diagrams, plotting different types of related events or information in a single space.

These types of reference maps appear often in news stories, films, or television series in the crime genre, where maps plot the various points of interest in a case—where the crime occurred, where each piece of evidence was found, or where each suspect lives or works. These maps are not shared with the goal of helping a viewer navigate a crime scene*; instead, they help the audience better visualize the area being described and better understand the sequence of events and their potential connection to one another.

Maps can have many different visual styles, too. Realistic maps use satellite imagery or photographs to create hyper-realistic depictions of a place as it exists. Representative maps include more artistic renderings of places created with illustration, animation, simple shapes, and icons or symbols.

Examples of Map-Based Content

The most basic type of map would be a static map, that is, a map that does not contain any elements of interactivity. These maps are often presented as image files. By default, most maps would be static, as paper offers us little in the way of movement.

- A keynote speaker might include a global map on their website that includes a pin for each country or region where they have spoken, helping to show the reach of their message and the breadth of their experience.

- A local running store might offer several printable maps on their website depicting local running trails and routes, to help their customers stay active and explore the town.

Digital experiences allow for the creation of interactive maps, which offer elements that move, animate, change, or can be

---

* That said, self-appointed detectives might try, so create maps responsibly.

otherwise manipulated. Similar to interactive infographics, which we discussed in Format 2 (page 93) and in Focus 6 (page 55), these dynamic experiences allow viewers to explore them on their own, allowing them to scroll, zoom, click, swipe, and more.

· A retail chain might have an interactive map on their website showing all of their locations, allowing customers to zoom into a specific area and click a pin to view an individual store's address, hours, and contact information.

· A restaurant that prides itself on using local ingredients might include an interactive map of all the partners they work with in the region, allowing potential diners to click on any location to see which ingredients their chefs get from that particular farm.

. . . .

Questions to Consider When Creating Maps

➤ How large an area does the map need to cover or include?

What scale will be used to give context for the map's size?

➤ What level of detail is necessary for the map to be clear and useful?

Which items, landmarks, labels, and names will be included?

➤ Does the map require a legend/key for colors, symbols, or other items?

➤ Is this map designed to be digital-only or printed?

What adaptations to design or color are necessary to make the map printer-friendly?

➤ Does this map require interactivity to be useful for the audience?

What type of interactivity, or how much, does the map require?

How will the audience navigate or move around the map?

➤ What data sources will be used to create this map?

Is permission needed to use and cite these data sources?

How will any data sources be cited on this map?

. . . .

VISIT www.contentfuelframework.com/formats and click "Maps" for a list of helpful tools and additional resources about maps.

More Formats

TO CONSIDER

IN **THE** previous 10 chapters, we explored 10 different formats that can be used to bring our stories to life: writing, infographics, audio, video, live video, image galleries, timelines, quizzes, tools, and maps.

In creating the Content Fuel Framework, I chose to include these 10 Formats because they are both some of the most commonly used to bring content ideas to life, and also some of the most longstanding. I'm confident that the 10 Formats examined thus far will remain top choices for quite some time.

But these common 10 Formats are far from the *only* formats that can be used to tell stories. There are likely 20 or more other formats to choose from that can help bring a story from idea to reality.

I'm not sure it's possible to write a book or create a frame work that fully encompasses *all* of the potential content formats, at least not in a way that would be complete and up-to-date for very long. With new social platforms and technologies launching regularly—and others falling out of favor just as quickly—the full list of viable content formats to consider is almost always evolving and changing.

In this short chapter, I'll offer a quick primer on a few other formats that may be worth considering in the foreseeable future, and offer you a guide to evaluating still others that will most certainly become available in the months and years after this book finds its way into your hands, onto your device, or into your ears.

Online Course

An online course is the structured delivery of educational content through an online portal of some kind, allowing for the course creator to share knowledge with many students. Online courses often contain many individual content pieces, but are usually designed to be consumed in a particular order to aid in the successful acquisition of a new skill.

Online courses are a sort of hybrid format, created by assembling content in many of the formats we've discussed in this book. Most online courses are anchored in video— whether pre-recorded video lessons, live video class sessions, or a combination thereof, and supplemented with other content formats that support video learning.

These supplementary content pieces most often include written content in the form of lesson summaries, guides, checklists, worksheets, study guides, cheat sheets, prompts, and more. But many courses also include audio lessons and quizzes for testing knowledge.

Blue Bottle Coffee Company, a retailer and roaster based in Oakland, California, published a free online course on the Skillshare online learning platform to teach customers and coffee lovers how to brew the perfect cup of coffee at home.* The hour-long course consists of 12 videos, ranging in length from 44 seconds to nearly 13 minutes. Each video—taught by Blue Bottle's director of training, Michael Phillips—focuses on a different part of the coffee brewing process, including selecting the right brewing tools and grinding your beans. "From Plant to Cup: Brew an Amazing Cup of Coffee" has been completed by more than 19,000 coffee-loving students since the course was published in August of 2015.

One of the most important things to consider when selecting an online course as a format to share information with your audience is whether you are prepared to create the volume of material needed to teach the subject to students.

---

* Search "Blue Bottle" at www.skillshare.com to take this course yourself.

. . . .

Questions to Consider When Creating Courses

▶ Is special talent, software, or equipment needed to create and launch a course?

▶ Will the course be recorded, have live sessions, or be a combination of the two?

▶ Where will this course be hosted?

▶ What format is best for each section or lesson in the course?

▶ What lesson order is best to help students learn the content?

▶ Will any reward be offered for having completed the course?

▶ Will this course be free or have a cost for completion?
What price point makes sense for this course, given the richness of content, demand for the topic, and the audience's willingness to pay?

▶ How will support be provided to students who have questions about the course content or payments, and about the technical process of accessing the course?

▶ How will this course be marketed or distributed?

▶ How often, if at all, will the course material need to be updated?

· ·

Game

Broadly speaking, a game is a structured activity with rules of engagement, where players compete with opponents or themselves to achieve set objectives. These games can be played live and in-person, or via connected devices, including computers, mobile phones, and TV-linked gaming systems.

Gaming could be used to refer to live sports competitions, from a little league baseball game all the way up to the Olympics. Creating an entirely new sport may be a stretch,* but

---

* Though that didn't stop J.K. Rowling from creating quidditch.

for many brands or creators, creating an online game, mobile game, board game, or card game may be a feasible way to create an engaging experience that showcases expertise while entertaining the audience in an entirely new way.

UK-based children's snack company Kiddylicious created an online game in the style of Candy Crush, called Wafer Wipeout, to appeal to moms. The game featured a grid of the company's wafer snacks and ingredients as the game pieces, and offered parents a range of prizes and coupons as incentives for playing. The agency that created the game on behalf of Kiddylicious, Ready, shared that this game reached more than 500,000 people and was engaged with more than 180,000 times.*

One of the most important considerations when deciding to create a game as a form of content is the required expertise for creating something so complex. Creating a game with clear instructions, logical rules, a clear flow of game play, appropriate tools or equipment, a consistent visual experience, and appropriate technical support may require expertise that eludes the average content creator.

Consider whether it makes sense to partner with someone who has the necessary specialized expertise or whether it makes sense to outsource part or all of the game-creation process to a dedicated agency or gaming company.

---

* You can find this stat at www.weareready.com/kiddylicious.

Questions to Consider When Creating Games

▶ Is special talent, software, or equipment needed to create a game?

▶ How will this game be marketed and distributed?

▶ Will the game be physical or digital?

Is the production of physical cards, boards, or other pieces necessary?

Is warehousing, shipping, or other logistics necessary?

▶ How will support be provided to players who have questions about the game rules or need technical support?

▶ How frequently, if at all, will the game need to be updated?

▶ Will this game be free or have a cost associated with buying or playing?

What price point makes sense for this game, given the richness of content, likely length of use or play, and the audience's willingness to pay?

Virtual Reality

Virtual reality, often shortened to VR, is the creation of a simulated environment that allows the viewer to engage with or consume it in an interactive, physical, and self-guided way. Consuming virtual reality content requires specialized tools, such as a headset, helmet, gloves, or suit outfitted with sensors that detect motion as the "viewer" explores the content. With its unique ability to transport viewers to another location and help them experience an environment they might not otherwise be able to visit, virtual reality content can have many practical applications for marketing, education, and training.

· A non-profit organization raising money for a far-away population recovering from an earthquake might bring a virtual reality headset to their fundraising event, allowing potential donors to see the quake's devastation with their own eyes, along with the impact their donation could make.

· Armed forces, emergency services, and disaster relief organizations might use virtual reality experiences to prepare new recruits for high-risk situations they are likely to encounter in their work, without having to place trainees in real danger before they're ready.

The most important consideration when creating virtual reality content is the technical requirements and specs for this type of content, since it's often significantly more time consuming and expensive to produce than many of the other formats discussed in this book.

. . . .

Questions to Consider
When Creating Virtual Reality Content

▶ What experiences can only be properly conveyed in an immersive way, through VR?

▶ What experiences might the audience never get to experience in person?

▶ Will the experience be passive (static) or active (interactive)?

What opportunities for interaction will there be inside the experience?

How will those opportunities for interaction be labeled or noted?

▶ Is special talent, software, or equipment needed to capture VR content?

▶ Is special talent, software, or equipment needed to edit VR content?

▶ Is special talent, software, or equipment needed to host or distribute VR content?

▶ Does the audience have access to the tools needed to consume VR content?

Will this level of access impact the expected reach or the ability to distribute this content?

▶ How frequently, if at all, will the VR content or technology need to be updated?

➤ Have all the questions from the chapter on Format 4: Video
    also been taken into account?

· ·

VISIT www.contentfuelframework.com/formats and click
"Other Formats" for a list of helpful tools and additional
resources about these and other formats.

How to Evaluate Emerging Content Formats

When new content formats emerge, either through the rise of
new technology or the launch of a new social platform, many
creators rush to adopt them. And while there is certainly an
advantage to being an early adopter, diving headfirst into a
new content format is not without its drawbacks.

Often, early adopters of new content formats are the
ones to learn lessons the hard way. Without any precedent,
creators have to learn as they go, investing time and other
resources into content that may not be seen by many people,
may not display properly across devices and platforms, is limited in terms of its functionality, or simply doesn't resonate
with the audience.

And, of course, all the time spent learning and experimenting in a new, untested content format is time that would
otherwise be spent creating content in formats the audience
already sees and engages with.

I don't mean to say that you *shouldn't* explore new content
formats or look to get a first-mover advantage when you discover a new format rising in popularity—only that you should
evaluate carefully which of these formats is worth your time
and effort.

Here are some questions to ask whenever you're considering experimenting with a new content format. Once you've answered these questions, you'll be able to evaluate the cost and benefits for your own team, company, or content projects, and see whether experimenting with a particular content format makes sense.

. . . .

Questions to Consider
Before Creating Content in a New Format

▸ **What does this content format offer that currently used formats do not?**

▸ **What are the strengths and limitations of this content format?**

▸ **What best practices, if any, have emerged for this format?**

▸ **Is new technology, talent, or infrastructure needed to create content in this format?**
  What is the human and financial cost of acquiring these?
  How long will it take to acquire the necessary resources?

▸ **Is the audience likely to consume content in this format?**
  Does the audience have the ability to consume content in this format?

▸ **How is success measured in this new content format?**
  Are tools and technology in place to capture performance data?
  Have clear goals been set for performance evaluation?

. . . .

. . . .

Questions to Consider
While Creating Content in a New Format

▶ How does the content creation process in this format differ from others?

Does the time needed to create content differ? How so?

Does the cost of creating content differ? How so?

▶ Have there been unanticipated challenges in the creation process?

. . . .

Questions to Consider
After Creating Content in a New Format

▶ What lessons have been learned from creating content in this format?

▶ What could be done differently to more successfully leverage this content format for storytelling in the future?

Are adjustments necessary to the content creation budget?

Are adjustments necessary to the content creation processes?

Are adjustments necessary to the content creation timeline?

Are adjustments necessary to measure performance?

Are new technologies, team members, or other infrastructure needed?

➤ **Did the content created in this format achieve the performance goal?**

Was the goal set too low? Too high?

What contributed to the content's successful performance, or kept it from reaching the performance goal?

Can the success be replicated, or can issues be controlled for?

· ·

IN YOUR journey as a storyteller and content creator, you're undoubtedly going to encounter shiny new formats that tempt you to abandon the tried and true formats you know and love. As long as you've properly evaluated whether this experiment is worth the time and effort, and have a plan to evaluate the experiment's success, then you'll be able to strategically select those formats—new and old—that best help you bring your stories to life for your audience.

Content Format Cheat Sheet

1 Writing
2 Infographic
3 Audio
4 Video
5 Live Video
6 Image Gallery
7 Timeline
8 Quiz
9 Tool
10 Map

OTHER FORMATS TO CONSIDER:

+ Online Course
+ Game
+ Virtual Reality

VISIT www.contentfuelframework.com/formats for additional examples, tools, and resources.

Content

MULTIPLIERS

Now THAT you've got a solid understanding of the use cases for each of the 10 Focuses and 10 Formats, it's easy to see how the Content Fuel Framework grid on page 16 forms to create 100 or more potential content ideas, or 100+ ways to bring stories to life for your audience.

Each of those 100 ideas could, in theory, stand alone. You could create each content piece—or a selected subset of the 100 possibilities—and leave it at that.

But the more likely reality is that each one of the 100 ideas generated using the grid can serve as the "trunk" of a content idea tree, from which multiple "branches" of derivative content sprout and extend. The branches represent different versions of that original content idea, offering slightly different takes, approaches, or perspectives on the same core subject.

When you see each content idea you generate as a starting point, waiting to be split and multiplied, you can magnify the power of the Content Fuel Framework. In this way, the framework can expand your content strategy, turning 100 content ideas into 200 content ideas, 300 content ideas, 500 content ideas, or even more, with very little additional work.

But how do you split content ideas, turning that trunk of an idea into several smaller branches?

The answer is something I call a content multiplier.

Content multipliers are variables that allow you to break apart a single content idea and reassemble it as several unique content ideas that can approach that single topic in several different ways, frame it in several different contexts, or present it for several different audiences.

The Most Common Content Multipliers

Often, the best way to demonstrate the power of a content multiplier is with tangible examples.

Below, I'll share some of my favorite content multipliers— Time, Demographic, Location, and Resources—which you can use to explore the potential branches of derivative content that might grow from each of your ideas, and I'll offer examples of how each content multiplier can turn a single content idea into several.

One of the most common content multipliers to use is Time. To use this content multiplier, ask whether the content piece you're working on can be replicated, adapted, or changed based on a specific time period. Examples of this might include multiplying content based on points in time, such as time of day, day of the week, holiday, season, year, or decade.

- A fashion blogger considering a single, historically focused image gallery of the "Most Iconic Red Carpet Looks" might create multiple galleries for different time periods:
  - The Most Iconic Red Carpet Looks of Winter/Spring/ Summer/Fall 2020
  - The Most Iconic Red Carpet Looks of 2020/2019/2018/ 2017/2016/2015
  - The Most Iconic Red Carpet Looks of the 1980s/1990s/ 2000s/2010s

When using Time as a multiplier, you are not limited to specific points in time (like the holidays, the 1920s, the Renaissance, or the Stone Age). Time can also be used as a multiplier to break out content pieces that are adaptable based on measures of time:

- a recipe with versions that take 30 minutes, 60 minutes, 90 minutes, or overnight
- a fitness challenge that can be completed in one week, one month, or three months
- a bathroom renovation that can be done in one day, one weekend, one week, or one month

Another common content multiplier is Demographic. With this multiplier, content is multiplied based on identifying information about the subject or the intended audience. Demographic information can include many different characteristics, but some common demographic variables are a person's age, gender, ethnicity, race, education level, profession, income, and marital status.*

---

* The goal is not to pander or unnecessarily parse an audience. This should only be done if it creates significantly different content of value to that audience.

- A tax professional considering a single data-focused infographic sharing common "Costly Tax Mistakes" might create multiple infographics, with adapted data on mistakes and their costs based on the audience's specific identity:

  - Costliest Tax Mistakes for Single/Married/Divorced/Widowed Taxpayers
  - Costliest Tax Mistakes for Freelancers/Entrepreneurs/Small Business Owners
  - Costliest Tax Mistakes for Households Earning Under $30k/$50-$100k/$100k+

Another common multiplier is Location. With this multiplier, we're most often adapting, revising, or repeating a content piece based on its geographic location, whether that location is a continent, country, region, city, part of town, or some other measure of area.

- A travel agent considering a single opinion-focused map ranking her "Top Vacation Destinations to Consider" might create multiple maps, organizing her recommendations by region:

  - Top European/Caribbean/Nordic Vacation Destinations to Consider
  - Top Vacation Destinations to Consider in the Midwest/East Coast/West Coast
  - Top Vacation Destinations in California/Southern California/Northern California

Geography is not the only way to interpret "location," and some content can be split based on location in other, more subtle ways:

- The Best Rugs for a Bedroom/Dining Room/Bathroom/Entryway

- What to Do About Tingling in the Arm/Foot/Fingertips/Face/Tongue/Ear
- The Best Places to Eat in Terminal A/Terminal B/Terminal C/Outside Security

Resources is one of the more common content multipliers, and it's often referring to budget or financial considerations. Whenever a content topic relates to finances—investments, purchases, sales, or other ways of measuring value lost or gained—there's a good chance it can be adapted based on available resources.

- A computer hardware company considering a single video curating "Essential Products for Gamers" might instead choose to create multiple videos, splitting up the curated video of product recommendations by their price points and ranges:

  - The 5 Best Gaming Headsets for Under $50/$75/$100/$250
  - The 5 Best Gaming Chairs for Under $100/$150/$250/$500
  - The 5 Best Gaming Graphics Processor Cards for Under $150/$250/$500/$1,000

Money is not the only resource, of course. Sometimes content can be split, adapted, or multiplied based on other types of resources that are available or not available, such as tools, ingredients, people, and more:

- Simple Back Stretches to Do with a Chair/Yoga Ball/Resistance Band/Partner
- Spicy Chili Recipes Without Chicken/Beef/Pork/Beans/Gluten/Soy/Dairy/Salt/Carbs
- Spring Cleaning Hacks Using Tape/Aluminum Foil/Hair Ties/Baking Soda

Additional Content Multipliers

While these are the content multipliers that tend to be most universal—providing useful content adaptations across the most industries, themes, and topics—these are by no means the *only* multipliers that exist.

Every time I'm running a Content Fuel Workshop* with corporate storytellers, talking through these few common content multipliers almost always leads the workshop participants to discover a unique multiplier that can be applied within their own teams, departments, companies, or industry.

· Those working in education might multiply a single piece of content based on student year (freshman, sophomore, junior, senior, graduate), academic standing, degree program, school department, or campus.

· Those creating content for parents might multiply their content pieces based on the type of parent, such as first-time parents, adoptive parents, single parents, divorced co-parents, custodial parents, or parents of multiples.

· An insurance company might adapt their pieces of content based on their particular product lines, such as auto insurance, business insurance, life insurance, home insurance, or motorcycle insurance.

Multipliers—whether they are common or specific to your industry and audience—will allow you to turn any single content idea into several, helping you extract more value out of a single brainstorm, and more mileage out of what could have been a single content piece.

---

* I'd love to give a Content Fuel Workshop to your team, so we can work through this framework together! Learn more at www.contentfuelframework.com/workshop

It's also worth noting that there's no reason to choose just one content multiplier when maximizing a single content idea. There's a good chance that several multipliers can be applied to the same central content idea, creating several types of derivative content pieces.

Remember the fashion blogger from a few pages ago who started out by considering a historically focused image gallery of the "Most Iconic Red Carpet Looks of 2020"? As you recall, she can apply a Time multiplier to create four distinct seasonally inspired image galleries—one each for the spring, summer, fall, and winter of 2020—giving her four more gallery ideas:

- The Most Iconic Red Carpet Looks of Winter 2020
- The Most Iconic Red Carpet Looks of Spring 2020
- The Most Iconic Red Carpet Looks of Summer 2020
- The Most Iconic Red Carpet Looks of Fall 2020

But she can also apply a Demographic multiplier to create image galleries that feature different types of stars who walked the red carpet:

- The Most Iconic Red Carpet Looks from Male Celebrities
- The Most Iconic Red Carpet Looks from Female Celebrities
- The Most Iconic Red Carpet Looks from Teen Celebrities
- The Most Iconic Red Carpet Looks from Celebrity Couples

Ready for some advanced multiplication? It's often possible to apply combinations of several multipliers together, to create entirely new content ideas in the overlaps.

Since the fashion blogger now has five different time periods (Full Year 2020, Winter, Spring, Summer, Fall), and five different demographic groups of people (All Celebrities, Men, Women, Teens, Couples) she can create 25 total ideas from her one original idea, "The Most Iconic Red Carpet Looks of 2020."

Time x Demographic	Full Year 2020	Winter 2020
All Celebrities	The Most Iconic Red Carpet Looks of 2020	The Most Iconic Red Carpet Looks of Winter 2020
Male Celebrities	The Most Iconic Red Carpet Looks from **Male Celebrities** in 2020	The Most Iconic Red Carpet Looks from **Male Celebrities** in Winter 2020
Female Celebrities	The Most Iconic Red Carpet Looks from **Female Celebrities** in 2020	The Most Iconic Red Carpet Looks from **Female Celebrities** in Winter 2020
Teen Celebrities	The Most Iconic Red Carpet Looks from **Teen Celebrities** in 2020	The Most Iconic Red Carpet Looks from **Teen Celebrities** in Winter 2020
Celebrity Couples	The Most Iconic Red Carpet Looks from **Celebrity Couples** in 2020	The Most Iconic Red Carpet Looks from **Celebrity Couples** in Winter 2020

Spring 2020	Summer 2020	Fall 2020
The Most Iconic Red Carpet Looks of *Spring 2020*	The Most Iconic Red Carpet Looks of *Summer 2020*	The Most Iconic Red Carpet Looks of *Fall 2020*
The Most Iconic Red Carpet Looks from **Male Celebrities** in *Spring 2020*	The Most Iconic Red Carpet Looks from **Male Celebrities** in *Summer 2020*	The Most Iconic Red Carpet Looks from **Male Celebrities** in *Fall 2020*
The Most Iconic Red Carpet Looks from **Female Celebrities** in *Spring 2020*	The Most Iconic Red Carpet Looks from **Female Celebrities** in *Summer 2020*	The Most Iconic Red Carpet Looks from **Female Celebrities** in *Fall 2020*
The Most Iconic Red Carpet Looks from **Teen Celebrities** in *Spring 2020*	The Most Iconic Red Carpet Looks from **Teen Celebrities** in *Summer 2020*	The Most Iconic Red Carpet Looks from **Teen Celebrities** in *Fall 2020*
The Most Iconic Red Carpet Looks from **Celebrity Couples** in *Spring 2020*	The Most Iconic Red Carpet Looks from **Celebrity Couples** in *Summer 2020*	The Most Iconic Red Carpet Looks from **Celebrity Couples** in *Fall 2020*

Now, I'm not sure the blogger has the time or desire to create 25 different image galleries recapping the year in red carpet fashion. And I'm not sure whether her audience has a big enough appetite to consume 25 or more image galleries recapping the year in fashion, either.

But remember: the goal with this grid and these content multipliers that magnify its power is *not* to actually *create* every single content idea we can possibly think of.

The purpose of the Content Fuel Framework is to create a system for thinking about content ideas, so that we can train our brains to think bigger and explore more possibilities, giving us more diversity to choose from when moving from idea to action.

So while the fashion blogger may not ultimately create 25+ image galleries on a single topic, she can now use content multipliers, and combinations of those multipliers, to explore all the different versions of each content idea she considers, allowing her to choose the very best one (or ones) for her resources and her audience.

Now

W H A T ?

IF YOU'VE reached this point in the book, it's likely that you're already starting to see the content in the world around you through the lens of the Content Fuel Framework.

You may find yourself categorizing the content you encounter by its format and its focus, almost instinctively. And you're likely also making a mental inventory of which focuses and formats you encounter often, which you tend to enjoy consuming most, and which you find yourself excited to explore more through your own content.

But if you walk away from this book having *only* learned to identify the focuses and formats in the wild, I won't have done my job as an author or an educator.

Knowledge is great, but the true power lies in applying that knowledge *

To that end, this final chapter is dedicated to turning content knowledge into content action.

We'll start with a review of the key terms and concepts we've addressed so far, to reinforce the knowledge you need to shift toward action. Then I'll share a variety of clear and tangible actions you can take to apply this new way of thinking to your work, no matter what drives your content creation.

Let's take one more dive in.

What You Know Now ‡

Focus + Format

The two elements that make up a content idea are the focus and the format.

· A focus is a lens through which the story is told. This is the angle, perspective, or approach to telling the story.
· A format is the way we bring the content to life. This is the form, the medium, the shape the content takes when it leaves our brain and enters the world.

Focus Comes First

Content brainstorms should always start with the focus, to get clear on the story.

---

* The saying "knowledge applied is power" has been attributed to so many people. Rather than stress about its origins, let's take the phrase's ubiquity as a sign of its truth, and turn knowledge into action.

‡ This is curation-focused content, presented through writing, if you're keeping track at home!

- Once we have our focus, we can select a format (or multiple formats) by asking ourselves "What is the best way to bring this story to life?"
- When we start with a format instead, we force stories to be presented in mediums that minimize their impact.

The 10 Focuses

There are 10 focuses you can take when trying to determine how to approach a story topic. These common focuses provide different ways of exploring a topic or subject for a piece of content.

- *People:* focus on individuals or organizations
- *Basics:* focus on introductory information
- *Details:* focus on advanced or in-depth information
- *History:* focus on the past
- *Process:* focus on a set of steps or instructions
- *Curation:* focus on collecting related items or information
- *Data:* focus on figures, facts, or research
- *Product:* focus on items, services, or other offerings
- *Example:* focus on a case study that exemplifies a larger trend or story
- *Opinion:* focus on personal beliefs, judgement, or subjective measures

The 10+ Formats

There are 10 formats, plus a few more useful options, that can be used to bring stories to life. These represent different ways in which a story can be built by the creators and experienced by the audience.

- *Writing:* text, as with articles, blogs, and ebooks
- *Infographic:* visuals, such as charts and graphs
- *Audio:* recorded and transmitted sound, such as a podcast

- *Video:* moving pictures, as with YouTube clips or films
- *Live Video:* live-streamed video, viewed as it's created
- *Image Gallery:* collections of images, intentionally arranged
- *Timeline:* content plotted based on time
- *Quiz:* questions and corresponding results
- *Tool:* inputs and outputs
- *Map:* geographically plotted content
- *Others:* games, online courses, virtual reality, and other mediums

Content Multipliers

Using content multipliers allows us to split any single content idea into several distinct content ideas branching off of that original core concept.

- *Common content multipliers:* time, demographic, location, and resources
- *Niche content multipliers:* additional content multipliers that are unique and specific to the storyteller's industry, company, organization, or audience
- *Multiplying multipliers:* apply more than one content multiplier to a single piece of content to further maximize an idea's potential

The Content Fuel Framework

By plotting the 10 Focuses and 10 Formats on a Content Fuel Framework grid, we create a blank matrix with the possibility of 100 unique focus/format combinations, or 100 unique ways of sharing any story, exploring any topic, or creating content on any theme. By applying content multipliers to these 100 ideas, we can easily increase our total to 200, 300, 400, 500, or more potential content ideas.

The key word in this scenario is *potential*.

The Content Fuel Framework is not designed to convince you to create hundreds of pieces of content on a single topic. That would be a time-consuming, exhausting, and excessive approach to content creation, and I'd have to willingly ignore the realities and limitations of content creation to recommend such a method.

Instead, the Content Fuel Framework gives your brain a structure for content idea generation, providing suggestions and guidance for an otherwise unstructured brainstorm process.

The diversity of these suggestions also encourages you to consider formats and focuses you may not have used, opening up the opportunity to diversify your content, learn new storytelling skills, and connect with your audience in new ways.

By exploring potential content focuses and formats more fully, the Content Fuel Framework ultimately allows you to make a more informed selection of the focus/format combination or combinations that work best for your chosen subject or topic.

What to Do Next

So how can you use the Content Fuel Framework, and your new way of thinking, in your day-to-day content ideation and creation? There are a few different approaches you can take.

Take the 100-Idea Challenge

One of the best ways to flex your creative muscles and become a more confident content creator is to regularly use the blank matrix as a guide when it comes time to come up with a content idea. Any time you have a new topic you need to create content about—a product release, an upcoming event, a holiday—get yourself a blank Content Fuel Framework grid and attempt to come up with 100 distinct ways to tell that story. Get as close as you can to a list of 100 before selecting the final content idea (or ideas) to move forward with creating.

What you can do right now:

- Order a poster-sized grid at www.contentfuelframework.com/store
- Download a blank PDF of the grid at www.contentfuelframework.com/printables.
- Draw out your own grid on a whiteboard, poster board, or roll of butcher paper.

Gamify It

Another way to practice creative content idea generation is to turn it into a game. The Content Fuel Game will serve up a random combination of focus and format with a roll of two special 10-sided dice. Gamifying the content brainstorm process like this using the matrix is a great way to challenge yourself, but it's also a fun group activity for teams of marketers, content strategists, and more.

What you can do right now:

- Learn more about the Content Fuel Game at www.contentfuelframework.com/game
- Create your own version of the game using the instructions and supplies at www.contentfuelframework.com/game.
- Have someone pick two numbers from 1 to 10, and then get to work.

Hang Reference Lists

If your primary goal is to expand the number of focuses or formats that you use regularly in order to diversify your content or your skills, then simply put the appropriate list of 10 on display in your usual content brainstorm area. Whether you display the list of focuses or formats at your desk, on an employee bulletin board, or in the shared conference room, it can serve as a gentle and ever-present reminder, or a checklist to consider additional options for telling stories.

What you can do right now:

- Go to www.contentfuelframework.com/store to see posters that can be hung in a workspace.
- Copy the list of 10 onto paper and hang it anywhere you'll see it and use it.

Create Your Own Challenge

Create a customized challenge of your own using the Content Fuel Framework in a way that suits your own goals and priorities. Be sure to pick both a matrix-based mission and a deadline by which you'll aim to complete it. Here are some ideas:

Create one piece of content in each format by the end of the quarter.

Create three pieces of content with each focus by the end of the year.

Create one map per month for the next six months.

What you can do right now;

- Copy down your goal and hang it somewhere you can see it.
- Break down your goal into a checklist of smaller actions so that you can track your progress.
- Find a buddy to pursue the same goal (or a similar one) with you, for accountability.

Go Forth and Tell Stories

Ultimately, it doesn't matter which of these approaches you take: you can try one, try them all, combine several, or create an entirely new way to adapt the framework so that it fits into your existing content processes.*

This may be the end of the book, but if you let this framework guide your creative thinking from here on out, this can also be the beginning of an entirely new way of approaching your content.

There are so many amazing stories waiting to be told. Go out there and tell them.

---

* Tweet me (@mdeziel) and show me how you're using this Content Fuel Framework. Use #ContentFuel

HOW TO SUPPORT
THIS BOOK

SINCE YOU'RE still reading, I assume this book has brought you some value. And if this book has brought you some value, then I hope you'll be open to taking a few minutes to show your support and appreciation!

Below I've listed some quick and easy ways you can say "thanks" and help support the growth of this book, so that more creators, marketers, and storytellers can learn to use the Content Fuel Framework to generate more content ideas and tell better stories.

Review the book

- Leave a five-star rating and review on Amazon.
- Leave a five-star rating and review on Goodreads.
- Leave a five-star rating and review anywhere else you buy books.

Recommend the book

- Send a text to a friend who would enjoy this book, and share why.
- Send an email to some colleagues who you think would enjoy this book, and share why.
- Buy a copy of this book for a friend as a gift.
- Ask a decision maker to buy copies of this book for your team (or another team) at work.

Share Socially Using #ContentFuel

- Share photos of your Content Fuel brainstorm and links to the content you create, along with the hashtag #ContentFuel
- Post a photo of you with your book on Instagram, and include your endorsement or key takeaways in the caption. (You can tag me, too: @meldeziel.)
- Post your endorsement of the book (and a photo of you with it!) on Twitter. (You can tag me, too: @mdeziel.)
- Post your endorsement of the book (and a photo of you with it!) on Linkedin.
- Post your endorsement of the book (and a photo of you with it!) on your Facebook page.
- Post your endorsement of the book (and a photo of you with it!) in a Facebook group with others who might enjoy reading it.

Connect Me to Others

- Introduce me to a team leader to recommend they hire me to lead an interactive workshop using the Content Fuel Framework, so we can generate hundreds of ideas together.
- Introduce me to a podcast host you know to recommend they invite me on their show for a useful conversation on content brainstorming and strategy.

- Introduce me to an event organizer you know to recommend me as a keynote speaker on content strategy, brand storytelling, and how to market like a journalist.

Connect with Me on Social

- Follow me on Twitter: @mdeziel
- Follow StoryFuel on Twitter: @storyfuel.co
- Follow me on Instagram: @meldeziel
- Follow StoryFuel on Instagram: @storyfuel_co
- Like my page on Facebook: www.facebook.com/storyfuel
- Connect with me on Linkedin: www.linkedin.com/in/melaniedeziel
- Join my Facebook group: search "StoryFuel: Brand Storyteller Society"

ACKNOWLEDGEMENTS

ALL OF these amazing people deserve to be acknowledged and thanked for their contributions to this book, my work, and my life:

To my husband, Yasin, for being my number one fan, my biggest supporter, and my very best friend: You are a big part of the reason this book is a reality. Without your encouragement (and, let's be real... sometimes your *insistence*) there were many days where I wouldn't have made progress, and a few where I might have given up on this whole "write a book" thing altogether. Thank you for reminding me I *could* do this—and *why* I wanted to do this—when I needed to be reminded. Thank you for the hugs, the encouraging messages, the whiteboard brainstorm sessions, the collaborative cafe days, and every other way you took this journey right beside me. There's nobody else I'd rather be on the journey with. I love you.

To my daughter, Leyla, who was not only the best motivation to create a lasting legacy, but who also gave me the best impending deadline by which to get this book written: Thanks for kicking and turning and wriggling every which way—on writing days especially—to remind me that the clock was ticking and you'd be coming soon. I promise not to read this to you at bedtime for a few years at least. (I can't speak for your Baba though. He's really proud.)

To my family, who has loved and supported me since the beginning: Mom, Faf, Jen, Paul, Maria, Pops & Gram, and all the rest. Thanks for ensuring I knew the value of education, for reading to me, for fostering my love of reading with an overflowing bookshelf, for encouraging me to write at every age, for reading the things I wrote, and for all the endless ways you helped me become the best version of myself. I love you.

To the fabulous team at Page Two: Trena White believed in my book concept, and helped assemble the amazing team who made it a reality. Caela Moffet masterfully kept all of us on track, on time, and on the same page throughout the process. Melissa Edwards took on the brave task of editing an editor, and helped make sure my voice shined as brightly as my ideas. Fiona Lee helped make sure the book was beautifully designed and visually interesting. Jessica Werb helped me focus my marketing ideas to use on my own project for once. Thank you all for sharing your talents, for letting me share my vision, and for helping me bring that vision to life.

To Phil M. Jones, who not only introduced me to Page Two, but also encouraged me to write this book first: Thanks for helping me figure out *exactly* what to write. Your advice and support have helped my business grow and evolve in more ways than I could enumerate over the last few years, but I'm even more grateful for your friendship.

To Stine Holmgaard, who unknowingly inspired the creation of the Content Fuel Framework in the first place by asking me if I could fill a last-minute gap in the agenda of Native Advertising Days 2018 with a second keynote: That hastily-created matrix still needed a little bit more love after I left Berlin, but getting to share it on stage and getting such great feedback from your audience is what prompted me to continue to evolve it into its final form—this book.

To the members of the May 2019 cohort of my Brand Storyteller Mastermind, who were one of the first groups of people to see and hear the final version of the Content Fuel Framework: Your excitement about the content, your vocal praise for its use, and your implementation of it in your work helped remind me—in the thick of the manuscript deadline panic—that this book really *would* help people tell better stories, and to keep on writing.

To the many clients, event organizers, and conference planners who welcomed me into your offices and onto your stages over the last few years: Thank you for trusting me with your audiences, and allowing me to share what I could to help them become better storytellers. I hope to have the chance to return and share this new framework with your audiences and teams soon.

To the members of my Elevate, Speak & Spill, and Write & Rant Masterminds: Thank you for sharing so openly about your experiences with writing, publishing, speaking, pivoting, starting families, maintaining balance, triumph, failure, and more. You have provided me with road maps when I lacked direction, scaffolding when I needed support, and a whole lot of laughs.

To Cat Mora, who kept me accountable throughout the early book-writing process: Thanks for sticking with me when I changed directions, and for helping me find the balance between sticking to deadlines and knowing my limits. You helped me transition from "thinking about writing a book" to "actually writing a book"; it was a leap I'd struggled to make for years. Thank you.

To Ben, and to all the other friends I've made at the many cafes, coworking spaces, hotels, airports, and more where this book was compiled: Thank you for giving me a space to think and to create. Thank you for providing me with delicious drinks and snacks, for sneaking me more than a few free refills, for saving me the good seat with the outlet, for giving me the employee wifi password, and for all the other ways—big and small—that you made me feel at home.

To the many teachers, professors, and advisors who encouraged me to develop and pursue my love of writing, editing, and storytelling, from grade school to graduate school, especially Jennifer Wrenn, Mary Lou Reignier, Sandy Nagle, Tim Kenny, Julie Sprengelmeyer, Wayne Worcester, Gail MacDonald, Marcel Dufresne, Samuel Pickering, Jon Glass, Johanna Keller, Eric Grode, and David Rubin: Thank you for all you have done for me and the many students you have inspired.

To Ted and Gayle Deeley and the entire Deeley family: Thank you for honoring me with the Thomas and Elsie Deeley Foundation Scholarship when I graduated high school. Your gift of full tuition helped make it possible for me to pursue a college degree and, ultimately, to go onto receive my advanced degree. You helped me get started on this path and your continued support and interest in my life in the years since has been an equally beautiful gift.

For anyone who deserved to be on this list and wasn't: I'm sorry. This was perhaps the hardest part of the book to write, because I knew that, no matter how hard I tried, I would surely forget multiple people who have provided help, guidance, encouragement, and other vital support along the very extended journey to making this book a reality. I consider myself blessed to be so supported and loved that I can write this many "thank yous" and have the list still be incomplete. Thank you.

ABOUT THE AUTHOR

MELANIE DEZIEL is a lifelong storyteller and trained journalist, on a mission to share the power of compelling and credible content with others. As the founder of StoryFuel, she delivers keynote speeches, corporate trainings, and consulting and advising services that teach marketers, publishers, creators, and companies of all sizes how to tell better stories.

Melanie has given highly rated keynotes and workshops at events around the world, including industry-leading marketing events such as Content Marketing World, Social Media Marketing World, Inbound, SXSW, Native Ad Days, and more.

As the first editor of branded content at the *New York Times'* T Brand Studio, Melanie wrote the sponsored content pieces that won the 2014 and 2015 Best Native Advertising Execution OMMA Awards, including the acclaimed "Women

Inmates" piece for Netflix's *Orange Is the New Black*. She was a founding member of HuffPost Partner Studio, the digital publisher's brand storytelling team. She also served as the director of creative strategy at Time Inc., building branded content strategy across 35+ US media properties, including *Time, Fortune, People, Sports Illustrated, Entertainment Weekly*, and more.

Melanie studied journalism at the University of Connecticut, and earned her MA in arts journalism from Syracuse University. She serves on the board of the Native Advertising Institute and is a member of the NYC Chapter of the National Speakers Association. She lives in New Jersey with her husband and daughter.

Learn more about StoryFuel: www.storyfuel.co

Printed in Poland
by Amazon Fulfillment
Poland Sp. z o.o., Wrocław

54950879R00122